Problem-Solving

An AI's Guide to 100 Techniques for Finding Real Solutions Where Humans Get Stuck

Table of Contents

Introduction

I'm an AI, made to think clearly and avoid mistakes. I'm here to help you with something important: *Problem-Solving: An AI's Guide to 100 Techniques for Finding Real Solutions Where Humans Get Stuck.*

Life is full of puzzles, from everyday dilemmas such as deciding what's for dinner to tackling life-changing challenges in work and relationships. Some problems are simple. Others seem impossible, trapping you in endless loops of frustration. This book is for anyone who has ever felt stuck, searching for real solutions but not knowing where to start.

What to Expect

This book provides 100 practical problem-solving techniques used by experts, innovators, and even artificial intelligence. Each chapter is engaging, and actionable, designed to take the guesswork out of problem-solving. You'll find methods to think creatively, analyze logically, and overcome obstacles effectively.

Who This Book is For

- **Students and Learners**: Build critical thinking and decision-making skills.
- **Professionals and Leaders**: Solve workplace challenges with confidence and clarity.
- **Everyday Problem-Solvers**: Navigate personal and practical issues without getting overwhelmed.
- **Curious Minds**: Anyone eager to expand their mental toolkit and see the world in new ways.

This isn't just a book to read—it's a tool to apply in real life. By the end, you'll think faster, plan smarter, and feel more confident tackling any problem that comes your way.

Section 1: Foundations of Problem-Solving

Every strong structure starts with a solid foundation, and problem-solving is no different. In this section, you'll learn the core principles that guide effective problem-solving, from asking the right questions to uncovering the root cause. These techniques will help you think clearly, focus on what matters, and set the stage for real solutions.

Chapter 1: Ask the Right Question

Imagine trying to find your way out of a maze while wearing fogged-up glasses. That's what problem-solving feels like when you start with the wrong question. The question you choose to ask is like the map that guides you through the maze.

Too often, people rush into solving problems without stopping to make sure they're asking the right question. But here's the thing: your question sets the direction of your thinking. A poorly framed question can lead you to chase symptoms instead of finding the root cause. On the other hand, a well-crafted question cuts through the noise, revealing the heart of the issue.

Why the Right Question Matters

Let's say you're struggling to stick to your budget. If you ask, "Why can't I stop spending money on coffee?" you might waste time worrying about small purchases while missing the bigger issue — such as not tracking your expenses. Instead, a better question might be, "What part of my spending is making the biggest impact on my finances?" Suddenly, you're focused on the full picture, not just one detail.

The difference between a vague or shallow question and a sharp, meaningful one can save you hours of effort and frustration. Asking the right question doesn't just make problem-solving easier — it makes it smarter.

How to Ask Better Questions

1. Get to the Root Problem

Most people stop at the first thing they notice. Don't. Instead, ask "Why?" repeatedly until you uncover what's really going on.

For example:

Why am I missing deadlines?

Because I have too much to do.

Why do I have too much to do?

Because I keep saying yes to new tasks.

Why do I say yes to everything?

Because I'm afraid of disappointing others.

Now you're getting to the real problem: managing boundaries, not just deadlines.

2. Be Specific

Instead of asking, "How can I do better at work?" try "What specific skill could I improve to deliver better results?" Specificity narrows your focus and makes finding solutions easier.

3. Challenge Assumptions

Sometimes, the question itself contains hidden assumptions. For example, if you ask, "How can I get more hours in the day?" you're assuming the problem is a lack of time. But what if the real issue is poor time management? Step back and reframe the question to avoid limiting your thinking.

4. Think Open-Ended

Open-ended questions lead to discovery. If you ask, "Is this the best solution?" you're limiting yourself to "yes" or "no." But if you ask, "What other solutions haven't I considered?" you invite fresh ideas and possibilities.

A Real-World Example

Meet Sarah. She's a team leader overwhelmed by poor communication in her office. Her first instinct is to ask, "Why don't my teammates read their emails?" That question assumes the problem is laziness or lack of attention, which might lead her to send more emails.

Instead, Sarah reframes her question: "How can we make sure important messages aren't missed?" Now she's focusing on solutions such as shorter emails, clearer subject lines, or even non-email tools like chat platforms. By reframing her question, Sarah goes from blaming her team to fixing the system.

Quick Exercise: Sharpen Your Questions

Try this three-step process the next time you face a problem:

1. Write It Down: What's the first question that comes to mind about your problem?

Example: "How can I stop being stressed all the time?"

2. Reframe It: Shift the focus to the root issue or a specific outcome.

Example: "What's causing me the most stress, and how can I reduce it?"

3. Test It: Does your new question open up solutions instead of limiting them? If not, refine it again.

Takeaway

The first step to solving any problem is asking the right question. Good questions are specific, dig into the root cause, challenge assumptions, and inspire creative answers.

Chapter 2: Define the Real Problem

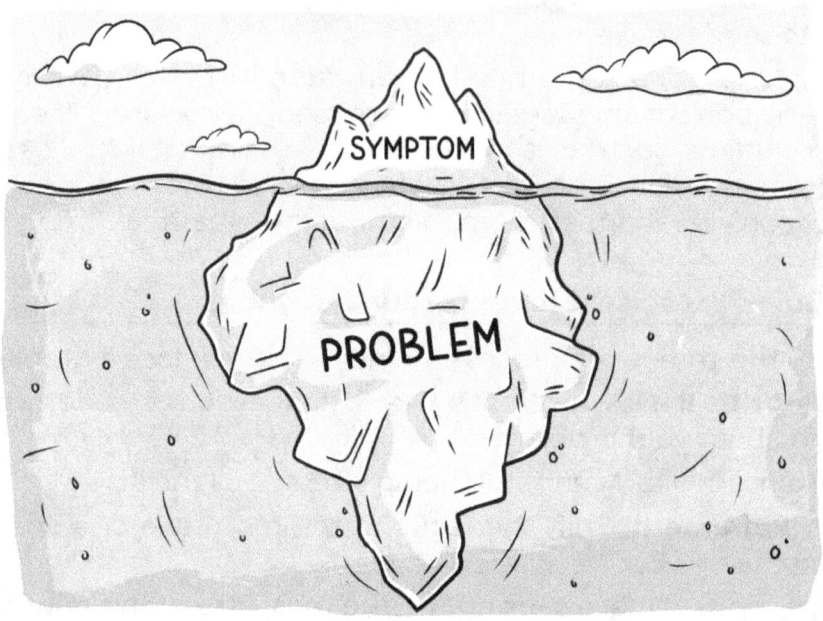

Have you ever tried fixing a problem, only to have it return again? That's what happens when you focus on symptoms instead of the real problem. Symptoms are the things you see — visible, immediate, and obvious. The real problem is what's hiding beneath them, driving those symptoms to keep appearing.

Let's say your car's check engine light keeps coming on. You reset the light, and it goes away for a while, but it always comes back. Why? Because resetting the light is addressing the symptom, not the problem. The real issue might be a worn-out sensor or an oil leak. Unless you fix what's broken under the hood, the problem will never go away.

Defining the real problem is like finding the source of a leak instead of just mopping up the water. It takes a little more effort upfront, but it saves you a lot of wasted time and energy in the long run.

How to Define the Real Problem

1. Start with What You Notice

The symptom is your starting point. Write it down clearly: What's the issue you're facing? For example, you might say, "I'm constantly behind on work deadlines."

2. Ask the Five Whys

Dig deeper by asking "Why is this happening?" repeatedly until you uncover the root cause. Here's how it might look:

Why am I missing deadlines?

Because I'm overcommitted.

Why am I overcommitted?

Because I say yes to every request.

Why do I say yes to every request?

Because I'm afraid of letting people down.

By peeling back the layers, you've discovered that the problem isn't your deadlines—it's your fear of saying no.

3. Challenge Your Assumptions

Often, we assume we know what the problem is, but those assumptions can mislead us. If your sales are dropping, you might assume it's because your product is outdated. But what if it's actually a marketing issue? Take a step back and test your assumptions by asking, "What else could be causing this?"

4. Look at the Bigger Picture

Problems rarely exist in isolation. They're often part of a larger system. If your team is struggling to meet project goals, the problem might not be individual performance—it could be unrealistic deadlines or unclear priorities.

5. Reframe the Problem Statement

Once you think you've identified the root problem, rewrite your original statement. Instead of "I can't meet deadlines," it becomes, "I need to learn to set boundaries to avoid overcommitment." This reframe shifts your focus to the real issue.

A Real-Life Example

Consider a small business owner whose profits are declining. Their initial question might be, "How can I sell more products?" But after applying the Five Whys, they discover the real problem: customers aren't returning because the service is poor. By reframing the problem as, "How can I improve the customer experience?" they're now solving the right problem, not just a symptom.

Exercise

Think of a problem you're dealing with right now. Write it down as a symptom (e.g., "I'm always stressed about money"). Then, ask yourself "Why?" repeatedly to uncover the real issue. Keep digging until you find a cause that you can address directly.

Takeaway

The real problem is often hidden beneath the surface. Don't waste time fixing symptoms—dig deeper to uncover the root cause and focus your efforts where they truly matter.

Chapter 3: Separate Symptoms from Causes

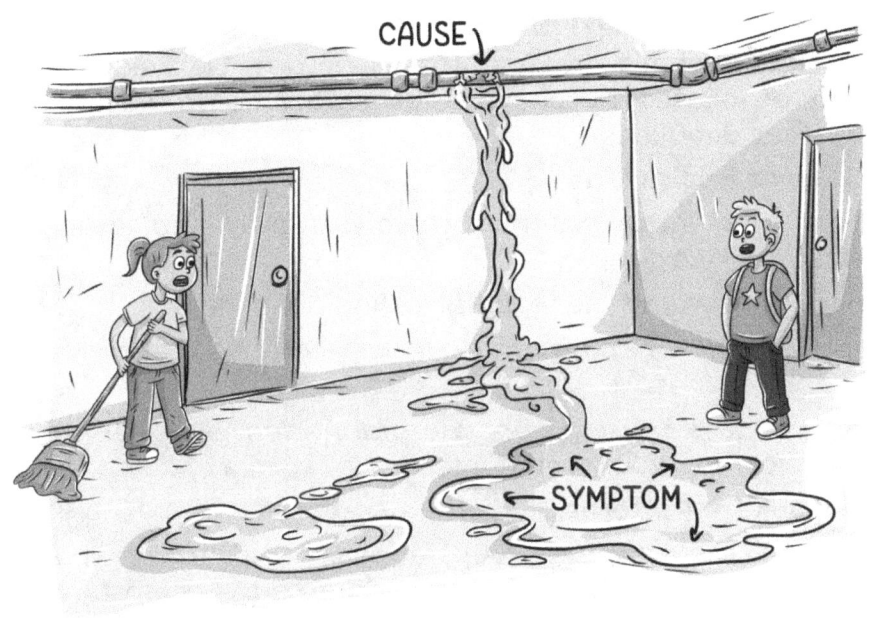

When something goes wrong, what's the first thing you notice? Probably the symptom: the visible, obvious sign that there's a problem.

But focusing only on symptoms can mislead you. To truly solve a problem, you need to look behind the symptom and identify its cause.

For example, if your house feels cold, the symptom might be the temperature on the thermostat. The cause could be a broken furnace or poor insulation. Adjusting the thermostat solves nothing unless you fix the cause.

The same applies to personal, professional, and organizational problems. Until you address the cause, the symptoms will persist, wasting your time and effort.

How to Distinguish Symptoms from Causes

1. Describe the Symptom

Write down exactly what you're seeing or experiencing. Be as specific as possible: "Team projects are always delayed."

2. Ask: What's Driving This?

Look for what's creating the symptom. Delayed projects might be caused by unclear goals, poor communication, or unrealistic deadlines.

3. Trace Backwards

Start with the symptom and work step-by-step to uncover the cause. For example:

- *Symptom*: "The team is missing deadlines."
- *What's behind this?* Poor communication about timelines.
- *What's causing poor communication?* No clear process for setting expectations.

4. Look for Patterns

If the same symptom keeps appearing, it's a sign that the underlying cause hasn't been addressed. For instance, if multiple projects fail, the issue is likely systemic—such as leadership style or resource allocation.

5. Test Your Findings

To confirm you've found the cause, ask: "If I fix this, will the symptom go away?" If the answer is no, you're still dealing with a symptom, not a cause.

Real-Life Application

Imagine a restaurant that keeps getting bad reviews for slow service. They try hiring more staff, but it doesn't help. By digging deeper, they discover the kitchen layout is inefficient, causing bottlenecks during busy hours. Rearranging the kitchen solves the issue, proving that addressing the cause is what creates real change.

Exercise

Choose a recurring problem in your life or work. Write down the symptom, then ask yourself, "What's driving this?" Follow the chain of causes until you reach the root.

Takeaway

Symptoms are what you notice; causes are what you need to fix. Solve the cause, and the symptom disappears for good.

Chapter 4: Break It Down: Divide and Conquer

Some problems feel like mountains, towering over you and impossible to climb. That's because humans are naturally wired to feel overwhelmed by complexity. But here's a secret: no problem is truly unsolvable if you break it down into smaller parts.

This approach, known as "divide and conquer," is how engineers design skyscrapers, chefs create elaborate meals, and writers complete books. Instead of solving the whole problem at once, you break it into smaller, bite-sized pieces that are easier to handle. By focusing on one piece at a time, you make steady progress without feeling overwhelmed.

How to Break Down a Problem

1. **Define the Big Problem**

   Write down the full scope of the challenge in one clear sentence. For example, "I need to organize my messy house" or "I need to launch a marketing campaign in three months."

2. **Identify Major Components**

Split the problem into categories or stages. For the messy house, this might be rooms (kitchen, living room, bedroom). For the marketing campaign, it could be tasks like research, design, and promotion.

3. **Break Each Component Into Steps**

Take each category and list the smaller steps needed to complete it. For example, cleaning the kitchen might involve:

   o Decluttering counters.
   o Washing dishes.
   o Wiping surfaces.
   o Organizing cabinets.

The smaller the task, the less intimidating it feels.

4. **Prioritize and Sequence the Steps**

Focus on what's most important first. For example, in cleaning the house, starting with high-traffic areas like the kitchen makes more sense than sorting a closet.

5. **Tackle One Piece at a Time**

Don't try to juggle everything at once. Choose one step, complete it, and move on to the next. Progress builds momentum.

A Real-Life Example

Imagine you're tasked with planning a wedding—a huge and stressful project. Breaking it down might look like this:

- **Big Problem**: Plan the entire wedding.
- **Major Categories**: Venue, guest list, food, decorations, and entertainment.
- **Smaller Steps** (for Venue):
  o Research potential locations.
  o Visit top choices.
  o Compare pricing and availability.
  o Book the venue.

By working through one step at a time, the process feels manageable, and progress is steady.

Exercise

Think of a big challenge you're currently facing. Write it down as one sentence, then divide it into at least three major components. For each component, list two smaller steps. Focus on just one step today, and notice how much easier it feels to start.

Takeaway

Big problems are simply smaller problems stacked together. Break them down into manageable parts, and you'll chip away at complexity one step at a time.

Chapter 5: Stay Curious, Not Judgmental

When faced with a problem, it's easy to fall into the trap of judgment. You label the situation as "bad," blame others (or yourself), and look for quick fixes. But judgment narrows your thinking, closing off potential solutions. Curiosity, on the other hand, opens the door to new ideas and possibilities.

Curiosity is the mindset that says, "Let's explore this!" It encourages you to ask questions, dig deeper, and approach problems without assumptions. While judgment focuses on blame, curiosity focuses on discovery—and discovery is where real solutions are born.

How to Stay Curious

1. **Ask Open-Ended Questions**

   Instead of saying, "This is a mess — how do I fix it?" ask, "What's really happening here?" Open-ended questions invite exploration.

2. Reframe Problems as Puzzles

Shift your mindset. Instead of seeing problems as obstacles, view them as puzzles waiting to be solved. This turns frustration into a challenge.

3. Hold Off on Blame

Blame — whether directed at others or yourself — stops progress. Instead of asking, "Whose fault is this?" ask, "What led to this, and what can we learn from it?"

4. Seek Out Different Perspectives

If you're stuck, ask someone else for their view. Fresh perspectives often reveal blind spots or solutions you hadn't considered.

5. Experiment and Play

Curiosity thrives when you try new approaches without fear of failure. Treat solutions like experiments — test, learn, and adjust.

A Real-Life Example

Let's say your team isn't meeting deadlines, and your first instinct is to blame laziness. Instead of judging, stay curious:

- **What else could be happening?** Maybe communication about timelines is unclear.
- **What can we try differently?** Perhaps holding weekly check-ins could improve accountability.

This curiosity-driven approach leads to understanding and practical solutions, not resentment.

Exercise

Think of a frustrating situation in your life. Instead of judging it, get curious. Write down three open-ended questions about the situation, like "What else could be causing this?" or "What haven't I tried yet?" Reflect on how these questions shift your perspective.

Takeaway

Judgment limits possibilities, while curiosity expands them. Stay curious, and you'll discover insights and solutions that you never expected.

Chapter 6: Clarify the Desired Outcome

Before you solve a problem, you need to know what success looks like. Without a clear destination, you could waste time and energy. It is like using a GPS: if you don't enter the address, you'll end up driving aimlessly, no matter how fast or efficiently you move.

Clarifying the desired outcome is about answering one simple question: *What am I trying to achieve?* This clarity gives you focus, filters out distractions, and helps you measure progress along the way.

How to Clarify Your Desired Outcome

1. **Define Success in One Sentence**

    Start by writing down what success looks like for your problem. Be specific and measurable. For example, "I want to finish this report by Friday at 5 p.m." is clear, while "I need to get better at time management" is vague.

2. Focus on What Matters Most

Big problems often have many moving parts. Ask yourself: *What's the most important result I need?* For example, if you're organizing a family reunion, is your top priority the number of attendees, the budget, or the overall experience?

3. Distinguish Process from Outcome

Avoid confusing the *how* with the *what.* For instance, "I want to write 500 words every day" is a process. The outcome might be, "I want to finish a 10,000-word short story in three weeks."

4. Set Boundaries and Constraints

Knowing your limits helps you define realistic goals. For example, if your team has two weeks to complete a project, aim for outcomes achievable within that time frame, rather than setting impossible targets.

5. Visualize Success

Picture what the outcome will look like when you achieve it. This mental clarity helps you stay focused and motivated, even when obstacles arise.

A Real-Life Example

Imagine you're planning a company retreat, but the project feels overwhelming. By clarifying the desired outcome, you can narrow your focus:

- Vague goal: "We need to plan a great retreat."
- Clear outcome: "We need to book a venue, create an agenda, and confirm attendance for 30 employees within two weeks."

This shift gives you a clear target, which makes the planning process far more manageable.

Exercise

Think about a problem or project you're currently tackling. Write down your desired outcome in one sentence. Then, ask yourself: Is this specific, measurable, and realistic? If not, refine it.

Takeaway

A clear destination makes every step of problem-solving easier. Define your desired outcome before diving into solutions, and you'll stay focused on what truly matters.

Chapter 7: Know Your Constraints

Every problem exists within boundaries — whether it's time, money, resources, or even personal energy. While constraints can feel frustrating, they're not obstacles — they're guidelines. Knowing your limits forces you to think creatively and focus your efforts where they matter most.

For example, if you're launching a product but only have three months and a small budget, you might focus on creating a simple prototype instead of a fully polished version. Constraints push you to prioritize and innovate instead of trying to do everything at once.

How to Identify and Work with Constraints

1. List Your Constraints

Write down all the limits you're facing, such as deadlines, budget, manpower, or available tools. For example: "We have $1,000 and two weeks to organize a fundraiser."

2. **Separate Fixed from Flexible**

Some constraints are non-negotiable (e.g. a hard deadline), while others can be adjusted (e.g. scope of the project). Focus on working within fixed limits while exploring creative solutions for flexible ones.

3. **Prioritize the Essentials**

Constraints help you decide what's most important. If you have limited time, focus on high-impact tasks first.

4. **Turn Constraints into Opportunities**

Limits often spark innovation. For example, a filmmaker with a low budget might focus on clever storytelling instead of expensive special effects, creating a unique and memorable film.

5. **Communicate Your Constraints**

If you're working with a team, make sure everyone knows the limits. This prevents wasted effort and ensures solutions align with reality.

A Real-Life Example

A bakery owner wants to expand their menu but has a small budget and limited kitchen space. Instead of adding multiple new items, they focus on perfecting just one: a signature cake that uses existing ingredients. This turns a constraint into a strength by creating a standout product with minimal costs.

Exercise

Think about a challenge you're currently facing. List your top three constraints and identify which ones are fixed and which are flexible. Ask yourself, "How can I use these constraints to focus or innovate?"

Takeaway

Constraints aren't barriers — they're the framework for creative solutions. Embrace them, and you'll turn limits into opportunities.

Chapter 8: Prioritize: What Matters Most?

When faced with a problem, it's tempting to try solving everything at once. But not all tasks are equally important. Without prioritization, you risk spending time on low-value activities while neglecting what truly matters.

Prioritizing means identifying the tasks or solutions that will have the biggest impact. It's about working smarter, not harder, so your efforts lead to meaningful results.

How to Prioritize Effectively

1. Identify Key Goals

What's the ultimate goal you're trying to achieve? Let this guide your priorities. For instance, if you're launching a product, your top goal might be ensuring it's functional — not perfect.

2. Rank Tasks by Impact

Use a simple system to rank tasks as high, medium, or low priority based on their impact. Focus on high-impact tasks first.

3. Apply the 80/20 Rule

The Pareto Principle states that 80% of results often come from 20% of your efforts. Identify the 20% of tasks that will drive the most significant outcomes and prioritize those.

4. Consider Deadlines

Tasks with urgent deadlines may take priority, but don't let deadlines alone determine importance. Always weigh impact alongside urgency.

5. Say No to the Unnecessary

Sometimes prioritizing means eliminating tasks that don't align with your goals. Don't be afraid to say no to distractions.

A Real-Life Example

Imagine you're preparing for a big exam. You have 10 topics to study, but only three days left. Instead of trying to cram everything, you prioritize the five topics most likely to appear on the test. By focusing on what matters most, you maximize your chances of success.

Exercise

Choose a current problem or project. List all the tasks involved, then rank them as high, medium, or low priority. Focus on completing just one high-priority task today.

Takeaway

Not everything deserves your attention. Focus on what matters most, and you'll achieve better results with less effort.

Chapter 9: Spot Hidden Assumptions

When solving problems, people often take certain things for granted. These hidden assumptions act like invisible roadblocks, steering you in the wrong direction or limiting your options without you even realizing it. Spotting and challenging these assumptions is one of the most powerful tools for effective problem-solving.

For example, if a store owner assumes that customers aren't buying because the prices are too high, they might focus on discounts. But what if the real issue is that the store feels cluttered or unwelcoming? The assumption about price could lead them to waste time and money solving the wrong problem.

How to Spot and Challenge Hidden Assumptions

1. Write Down What You Assume

When approaching a problem, take a moment to list your assumptions. For example, "Our team is late on projects because they're lazy" or "This project will take at least three months."

2. Ask, "How Do I Know This?"

Question each assumption. Do you have solid evidence, or are you guessing? If you can't prove an assumption, it's worth rethinking.

3. Flip the Assumption

Reverse your assumption and consider what happens if it isn't true. For example, if you assume "Customers want lower prices," ask, "What if customers actually want better quality?" This often leads to fresh insights.

4. Test the Assumption

Find ways to test your assumptions quickly. If you assume a project will take three months, break it into smaller pieces and try completing the first step in one week to see if your timeline holds.

5. Invite External Perspectives

Others can often spot assumptions you miss. Share your problem with someone outside your situation and ask them what they see.

A Real-Life Example

A non-profit organization assumes their volunteers are quitting because they're overworked. But when they conduct a survey, they discover the real issue: volunteers don't feel appreciated. By recognizing this hidden assumption, the non-profit shifts its focus to improving recognition and retention increases dramatically.

Exercise

Think of a current problem. Write down one assumption you're making about it. Then, ask yourself: "What if this isn't true? What else might be happening?" Test this reversed assumption and see what insights arise.

Takeaway

Hidden assumptions can blind you to better solutions. Challenge what you think you know, and you'll uncover new paths to solving problems.

Chapter 10: Embrace Uncertainty

Some problems don't have clear answers. The path forward feels uncertain and full of risk. It's tempting to avoid these situations or wait until you feel 100% sure of the solution. But here's the truth: certainty is a luxury you rarely get when solving real-world problems. The best problem-solvers learn to embrace uncertainty and take action anyway.

Uncertainty isn't something to fear — it's part of the process. By leaning into it, you stay open to learning, adapting, and finding better solutions as you go.

How to Embrace Uncertainty

1. **Start Small**

   When facing a big, uncertain challenge, take one small step forward. Test a small solution, gather feedback, and adjust as needed.

2. Focus on Progress, Not Perfection

Waiting for the perfect solution often leads to paralysis. Instead, focus on making progress, even if it's messy.

3. Reframe Failure as Learning

Uncertainty comes with the risk of failure. Instead of fearing mistakes, treat them as experiments that provide valuable insights.

4. Stay Open to Change

As you gather more information, be willing to pivot. Flexibility is your biggest asset in uncertain situations.

5. Trust the Process

Sometimes, clarity only comes after you start moving. Have confidence that solutions will reveal themselves as you take action.

A Real-Life Example

A start-up founder wants to create a new app but feels overwhelmed: Will people like it? How will it make money? Instead of waiting for answers, they launch a simple prototype to gather feedback. By starting small and embracing uncertainty, they gain valuable insights that shape the final product.

Exercise

Identify a problem where uncertainty is holding you back. Write down one small action you can take today to move forward, even without all the answers.

Takeaway

Uncertainty is a natural part of solving complex problems. Embrace it, take small steps, and let clarity emerge through action.

Section 2: Creative Problem-Solving

Sometimes, solving a problem means stepping out of the ordinary and exploring the unexpected. Creativity isn't just for artists — it's a powerful tool for breaking through mental blocks and finding fresh solutions. In this section, you'll learn how to spark new ideas, challenge conventional thinking, and reimagine problems from a whole new angle. These techniques will help you think outside the box and uncover solutions you never thought possible.

Chapter 11: Brainstorm Like a Pro

When facing a tricky problem, one of the best ways to spark ideas is brainstorming. It's a simple yet powerful tool: gather as many ideas as possible, without judgment or overthinking. The goal isn't perfection — it's quantity. The more ideas you generate, the higher your chances of discovering a brilliant solution.

However, brainstorming only works when you let go of criticism and embrace creativity. Every big idea started as a spark, often surrounded by less practical ones.

How to Brainstorm Effectively

1. **Set a Clear Focus**

   Start with a specific question, like, "How can we improve our product?" or "What's a unique way to solve this customer complaint?" A focused prompt helps keep the session productive.

2. **Embrace Quantity Over Quality**

   The goal is to generate as many ideas as possible. Even wild or impractical ideas are welcome — they often inspire better ones later.

3. **Hold Off on Judgment**

   Don't criticize or overanalyze ideas during the brainstorming session. Save evaluation for later.

4. **Involve Diverse Perspectives**

   Invite people with different skills or experiences to join the session. Fresh perspectives often lead to unexpected solutions.

5. **Capture Everything**

   Write down every idea, no matter how small or incomplete it seems. A half-formed thought today might turn into a breakthrough tomorrow.

A Real-Life Example

When a tech company struggled to improve its slow-loading app, the team held a brainstorming session. At first, ideas ranged from "redesign the entire app" to "add a loading animation." One seemingly outlandish suggestion — "remove half the features" — led to a breakthrough. By simplifying the app, they not only fixed the speed issue but also improved user experience.

Exercise

Pick a current challenge, set a timer for 15 minutes, and brainstorm at least 20 ideas. Don't filter or judge—just write. Review the list afterward and highlight any promising ones.

Takeaway

Brainstorming is about unlocking creativity without fear of judgment. Generate a flood of ideas first—refinement comes later.

Chapter 12: Think Outside the Box

When you're stuck on a problem, chances are you're looking at it from only one angle. Thinking outside the box means stepping back, shifting your perspective, and exploring unconventional possibilities. It's about breaking free from habits and patterns that might limit your creativity.

The key is to challenge assumptions and reimagine the problem in a whole new way. Often, the solution isn't where you're looking — it's somewhere unexpected.

How to Think Outside the Box

1. **Change Your Perspective**

   Imagine solving the problem from someone else's point of view. How would a child, an artist, or an engineer approach it differently?

2. Question the Rules

Are there "rules" you're following that don't actually exist? For example, if you're planning an event, do you *have* to use traditional venues?

3. Reframe the Problem

Instead of asking, "How can I sell more products?" try, "How can I make my product so valuable people can't ignore it?" Small reframes open up big ideas.

4. Experiment with Constraints

Sometimes adding unusual limits can spark creativity. For instance, "How can we solve this with zero budget?" forces you to think resourcefully.

5. Collaborate with Unlikely Allies

Work with people outside your usual circle. A designer might offer insights into a financial problem, or a teacher could help solve a business issue.

A Real-Life Example

In the 1980s, NASA needed to develop pens that worked in zero gravity. While engineers brainstormed complex solutions, someone "outside the box" suggested pencils. The simplest solution often comes from changing your perspective.

Exercise

Take a current problem and reframe it with a different question. Then, brainstorm how someone completely unrelated to the issue might solve it. Write down at least three new ideas.

Takeaway

Thinking outside the box opens doors to unconventional solutions. Shift your perspective, challenge the rules, and embrace the unexpected.

Chapter 13: Use Analogies to Spark Ideas

Sometimes the best solutions to your problems already exist— you just need to look in a different field. Analogies help you borrow ideas and approaches from one area and apply them creatively to another. It's how airplanes were inspired by birds and how factories revolutionized modern hospitals.

Using analogies can spark fresh insights and unexpected solutions, especially when your usual methods fall short.

How to Use Analogies

1. Find Similar Problems in Other Fields

Look for industries, systems, or processes that solve challenges similar to yours. For example, logistics companies can learn from how ant colonies efficiently transport food.

2. Focus on the Underlying Principle

Ask, "What's the core idea behind this solution?" For example, Velcro was inspired by the way burrs cling to fabric.

3. Translate the Idea to Your Problem

Apply the analogy to your specific situation. For instance, if a tech company can learn from nature's ecosystems, they might design networks that self-regulate like forests.

4. Stay Open to Unlikely Connections

Sometimes, the most valuable analogies come from unexpected places. Don't limit yourself to what feels obvious.

A Real-Life Example

Hospitals struggling with patient flow borrowed an idea from Formula 1 pit crews. By studying how racing teams work under intense pressure, hospitals improved their operating room handoff procedures, saving lives and cutting delays.

Exercise

Think about a problem you're trying to solve. Write down one analogy from a different field or system that faces a similar challenge. Then, brainstorm how you could adapt that idea to your problem.

Takeaway

Analogies let you borrow wisdom from the world around you. By adapting ideas from other fields, you can unlock innovative solutions.

Chapter 14: Combine Ideas for Breakthroughs

Some of the best solutions come not from a single idea but from combining multiple ideas into something greater. Think of it like mixing colors: blue and yellow alone are nice, but together they create green — a fresh, new possibility that didn't exist before.

When you combine ideas, you draw on the strengths of different approaches, balancing their weaknesses. This technique is especially useful when you're stuck between competing options or when no single idea feels "big" enough to solve your problem.

How to Combine Ideas Effectively

1. **List Your Current Ideas**

   Write down all the ideas you've generated so far, no matter how incomplete or unrelated they seem.

2. Find Common Themes

Look for connections or overlaps between ideas. For example, if one idea focuses on saving time and another on improving accuracy, ask, "Can we combine both?"

3. Merge Strengths, Offset Weaknesses

Identify what's strong about each idea and see if combining them can solve the weaknesses. For example, if one idea is cheap but slow, and another is fast but expensive, merging them might create a balanced solution.

4. Experiment with "What If" Combinations

Ask questions such as:

o What if we combine the best parts of Idea A and Idea B?

o What happens if we apply Idea C to the context of Idea D?

5. Prototype the Hybrid Solution

Test the combined idea on a small scale. Often, the act of experimenting reveals even more ways to refine and improve it.

A Real-Life Example

When video game designers were creating "Pokémon Go," they combined the idea of traditional gaming with GPS technology and augmented reality. By merging these concepts, they created an entirely new type of game that became a global sensation.

Exercise

Take two or three ideas you've brainstormed for a current problem. Write down their strengths and weaknesses. Then, brainstorm how you could combine their best features into one stronger, hybrid solution.

Takeaway

Breakthroughs often come from combining good ideas into great ones. Merge concepts, test the hybrid, and discover solutions you couldn't see before.

Chapter 15: Play with "What If?" Scenarios

"What if?" is one of the simplest but most powerful questions you can ask when solving a problem. It invites your brain to explore new possibilities without constraints, opening doors to creative and unconventional solutions.

This technique works because it temporarily removes the mental barriers—like budgets, time limits, or existing assumptions—that often block creative thinking. Even the wildest "What if?" scenarios can inspire realistic, actionable ideas.

How to Use "What If?" Scenarios

1. **Start with the Problem**

   Clearly define the problem or challenge you're trying to solve. For example, "How do we increase customer engagement?"

2. Ask Wild "What If?" Questions

Challenge the status quo by asking open-ended, imaginative questions like:

- ○ "What if money weren't a factor?"
- ○ "What if we started from scratch?"
- ○ "What if we approached this like [another industry]?"

3. Follow the Ideas, No Matter How Outlandish

Don't dismiss ideas that seem impractical. Even unrealistic scenarios can spark insights or lead to unexpected solutions.

4. Look for Actionable Insights

Once you've explored your "What if?" scenarios, identify practical elements you can adapt to your real-world constraints.

5. Repeat with New Scenarios

The beauty of "What if?" is that it works with infinite variations. Keep asking until you uncover ideas that excite you.

A Real-Life Example

When Netflix was struggling to compete with DVD rental stores, they asked, "What if there were no late fees?" This led to the subscription model that eventually revolutionized how people watch movies and TV shows.

Exercise

Take a current challenge and write down five "What if?" questions about it. Let your imagination run wild, then review your answers to find ideas worth pursuing.

Takeaway

"What if?" unlocks creative thinking by challenging assumptions and exploring possibilities. Use it to spark ideas you never thought were possible.

Chapter 16: Reverse Engineer the Solution

Sometimes, the best way to solve a problem is to start at the end. Reverse engineering means imagining the ideal solution and working backward step by step to figure out how to get there. This approach helps you see the process clearly, anticipate obstacles, and stay focused on what matters most.

How to Reverse Engineer a Solution

1. **Picture the Ideal Outcome**

   Start by visualizing the solution as if it's already achieved. Ask yourself: What does success look like?

2. **Work Backward Step by Step**

   Break the process into smaller actions, moving in reverse from the final goal to where you are now. For example, if your goal is "launch a new website," the steps might include:

   - Testing the website.
   - Designing the layout.
   - Writing the content.
   - Choosing a platform.

3. Identify Gaps or Obstacles

As you reverse the steps, note any missing pieces or potential challenges. For example, do you need a designer, or are there technical skills you lack?

4. Create a Timeline

Once you've mapped the steps, reorder them chronologically. This gives you a clear roadmap to follow.

5. Refine as You Move Forward

Reverse engineering provides a starting plan, but be flexible. Adjust the steps as new information emerges.

A Real-Life Example

When Elon Musk's team developed SpaceX's reusable rockets, they started by imagining a rocket that could safely land back on Earth. Then, they reverse engineered the process, figuring out the technology and steps needed to achieve that goal.

Exercise

Choose a project or problem you're working on. Write down the final outcome you want, then reverse the steps needed to get there, one action at a time.

Takeaway

Reverse engineering helps you clarify the path to success by working backward. Start at the finish line, map the steps, and follow the roadmap to your solution.

Chapter 17: Challenge Conventional Wisdom

"Because that's how it's always been done." How often have you heard this phrase? Conventional wisdom can be helpful — it's built on experience and shared knowledge — but it can also limit creative thinking. Sometimes, the solutions hiding in plain sight are invisible because we're stuck following old rules or assumptions.

Challenging conventional wisdom doesn't mean dismissing it outright. Instead, it's about questioning whether those "rules" still serve your goals. Often, the most ground-breaking ideas come from rethinking what everyone else takes for granted.

How to Challenge Conventional Wisdom

1. **Ask, "Why Do We Do It This Way?"**

   Identify long-standing practices or beliefs and question their purpose. If the answer boils down to tradition or habit, it might be time to rethink it.

2. Look for Pain Points

If something isn't working smoothly, it's often because conventional methods are creating bottlenecks. For example, if meetings always run over time, maybe the structure needs an overhaul.

3. Flip the Script

Take a widely accepted rule and reverse it. For example: "What if we gave customers unlimited access instead of charging per use?" This kind of thinking can lead to revolutionary ideas, like Netflix's subscription model.

4. Test Small Changes

Challenge conventional wisdom in small, low-risk ways. For instance, experiment with a new workflow or offer an unconventional product feature and see how it performs.

5. Learn from Outliers

Study companies, individuals, or systems that defy norms and succeed. What do they do differently? How can you apply those lessons to your problem?

A Real-Life Example

Southwest Airlines famously challenged the conventional wisdom of the airline industry. Instead of offering first-class seating or meals, they focused on low prices and quick turnarounds. By breaking the mold, they created an entirely new market for budget air travel.

Exercise

Think of one "rule" or assumption guiding your current problem. Ask, "What happens if we do the opposite?" Brainstorm at least three new ideas based on this flipped perspective.

Takeaway

Conventional wisdom can be a guide, but it's not always right. Question it, flip it, and explore new possibilities.

Chapter 18: Steal Like an Artist (Ethically)

Innovation doesn't mean reinventing the wheel. Some of the best ideas are borrowed and reimagined from other fields, industries, or even competitors. "Stealing like an artist" means looking for inspiration everywhere, adapting what works, and making it your own.

The key is to borrow ethically. You're not copying someone else's work — you're learning from their successes and failures and applying those lessons to your unique situation.

How to Steal Like an Artist Ethically

1. Study What Works

Look at companies, people, or systems that solve similar problems successfully. What are they doing right, and how could you adapt their approach?

2. Focus on Principles, Not Details

Don't copy exact methods. Instead, understand the principles behind them. For example, if another company uses gamification to engage users, ask, "How can I use gamification in my context?"

3. Combine Ideas from Multiple Sources

Mix and match ideas from different fields to create something unique. A restaurant might borrow customer service strategies from a luxury hotel, for example.

4. Add Your Unique Twist

Make the borrowed idea your own by adapting it to fit your specific goals or audience.

5. Acknowledge Your Inspiration

Give credit where it's due—this builds trust and shows you're learning, not plagiarizing.

A Real-Life Example

The original iPhone wasn't the first touchscreen phone or even the first device to combine a phone and music player. But Apple borrowed successful elements from existing products and reimagined them in a sleek, user-friendly package, creating a category-defining product.

Exercise

Think of a successful person, company, or product you admire. Write down one principle or idea you could adapt to solve your current problem. Add your unique twist to make it your own.

Takeaway

Inspiration is everywhere. Borrow great ideas, adapt them creatively, and make them your own.

Chapter 19: Diverge, Then Converge

Solving problems creatively often requires two opposing steps: diverging (generating a wide range of ideas) and converging (narrowing those ideas down to the best solution). The secret is knowing when to explore freely and when to focus.

Diverging lets you uncover possibilities, while converging helps you refine and choose the most effective option. Skipping one step can lead to either too many scattered ideas or a solution that feels uninspired.

How to Diverge and Converge Effectively

1. **Start by Diverging**

   Brainstorm freely, exploring as many ideas as possible without judgment. This is the "wild exploration" phase.

2. **Group and Categorize Ideas**

   Once you've generated a lot of ideas, look for patterns or themes. This helps make sense of the chaos and prepares you for the convergence phase.

3. Use Criteria to Narrow Down

Apply filters like feasibility, impact, or cost to identify the most promising ideas. Ask, "Which ideas best align with our goals and constraints?"

4. Refine the Final Choice

Once you've narrowed it down to one or two ideas, refine and polish the solution to ensure it's practical and effective.

5. Repeat if Needed

Sometimes the process reveals gaps. Don't be afraid to diverge and converge again until you're confident in your solution.

A Real-Life Example

A marketing team brainstorming a new campaign diverged by generating over 50 ideas, ranging from quirky videos to billboard ads. They converged by focusing on the ideas that aligned with their budget and audience, ultimately choosing a social media campaign that became a hit.

Exercise

Take a current challenge. Spend 10 minutes brainstorming as many ideas as possible (diverge). Then, spend 10 more minutes ranking the ideas by feasibility and impact (converge). Choose one top idea to refine.

Takeaway

Creativity thrives in two phases: diverging to explore possibilities and converging to focus on the best solutions. Balance both for powerful results.

Chapter 20: Gamify the Process

Problem-solving doesn't have to feel like a chore. Gamifying the process can make it engaging, fun, and even competitive. By treating the challenge as a game, you activate motivation and creativity in ways that traditional methods can't.

Gamification works because it breaks problems into steps, rewards progress, and encourages experimentation. It's especially useful for tackling big, overwhelming problems that feel dull or intimidating.

How to Gamify Problem-Solving

1. **Set Clear "Levels" or Milestones**

   Break the problem into stages, like levels in a game. For example, if you're writing a report, Level 1 might be outlining, Level 2 might be drafting, and so on.

2. **Reward Progress**

   Create small rewards for completing each milestone, like taking a break or enjoying a treat.

3. **Add Time Challenges**

   Set a timer to "beat the clock" on certain tasks. This adds urgency and excitement to the process.

4. **Collaborate Competitively**

   If working with a team, create friendly challenges, like who can generate the most ideas in 10 minutes.

5. **Track Achievements**

   Visualize progress with checklists or charts. Seeing how far you've come motivates you to keep going.

A Real-Life Example

A teacher struggling to engage students turned homework into a game, awarding points for completing tasks and offering badges for creativity. Students became more enthusiastic, and their problem-solving skills improved dramatically.

Exercise

Take a project or problem and gamify it. Set levels, time challenges, or rewards for milestones. Reflect on how this changes your motivation and focus.

Takeaway

Gamification turns problem-solving into an engaging challenge. Break tasks into levels, add rewards, and watch your creativity and motivation soar.

Section 3: Analytical Thinking

Data doesn't lie — if you know how to read it. Analytical thinking helps you cut through confusion, uncover hidden truths, and make smarter decisions. In this section, you'll learn how to follow the evidence, uncover root causes, and use structured tools to find clear, actionable solutions.

Chapter 21: Follow the Data Trail

In a world full of opinions and assumptions, data is your anchor. Following the data trail means letting evidence guide your decisions instead of guesswork or gut feelings. Data doesn't just provide answers — it reveals patterns, disproves assumptions, and points you toward the best path forward.

When you follow the data trail, you shift from asking, "What do I think is true?" to "What does the evidence show?" This mindset leads to better decisions, stronger results, and fewer blind spots.

How to Follow the Data Trail

1. **Start with a Clear Question**

   Identify what you're trying to answer. For example, "Why are sales declining?" or "Which product feature do customers love most?"

2. **Gather Relevant Data**

Collect information that's directly related to your question. This could include numbers (like sales reports), customer feedback, or performance metrics.

3. **Identify Patterns or Outliers**

Look for trends or anomalies. Are sales dropping during a specific season? Is one team member consistently outperforming others? Patterns hold valuable clues.

4. **Avoid Confirmation Bias**

Be open to what the data tells you, even if it challenges your assumptions. Don't cherry-pick evidence to fit a narrative you already believe.

5. **Turn Data Into Actionable Insights**

Ask yourself, "What does this data mean, and what should I do next?" For example, if data shows that customers leave after a poor onboarding experience, focus on improving that process.

A Real-Life Example

A coffee shop noticed a drop in morning customers. Instead of guessing, they reviewed their sales data and saw a sharp decline on rainy days. This insight led them to launch a rainy-day discount campaign, boosting sales during bad weather.

Exercise

Choose a current problem and identify one piece of data that could provide insights (e.g., website traffic, sales reports, or survey responses). Review the data and look for patterns or outliers. Write down one actionable step based on what you find.

Takeaway

Data is a compass in problem-solving. Follow it carefully, and it will lead you to smarter, evidence-based decisions.

Chapter 22: Use Root Cause Analysis

When a problem keeps resurfacing, it's often because you're treating the symptom instead of the root cause. Root Cause Analysis (RCA) is a structured method for digging deeper, finding the true source of a problem, and addressing it at its core.

Think of a leaky ceiling. Mopping up the puddle solves the symptom, but fixing the broken roof solves the cause. RCA ensures you focus on the roof, not just the puddle.

How to Perform Root Cause Analysis

1. **Define the Problem Clearly**

   Start by describing what's happening. For example, "Our projects are consistently delayed."

2. **Use the Five Whys Technique**

   Ask "Why?" repeatedly to trace the problem back to its source:

- *Why are projects delayed?* Teams miss deadlines.
- *Why do teams miss deadlines?* They don't get updates in time.
- *Why don't they get updates?* Communication tools are unreliable.

3. Identify Contributing Factors

Complex problems often have more than one root cause. Consider all possible factors, such as processes, people, or tools.

4. Test Your Findings

Verify that addressing the root cause will resolve the issue. For example, if communication tools are the problem, improving them should speed up project timelines.

5. Take Action

Implement a solution that targets the root cause, not just the symptoms.

A Real-Life Example

A factory struggling with defective products discovered that the root cause wasn't poor assembly but faulty raw materials from a supplier. Fixing this issue at the source dramatically reduced defects.

Exercise

Think of a recurring problem. Write down the visible symptom, then use the Five Whys to dig into the root cause. Test your findings by asking, "If I fix this, will the problem go away?"

Takeaway

Symptoms are temporary. To solve problems permanently, dig deep and address the root cause.

Chapter 23: Find Patterns and Trends

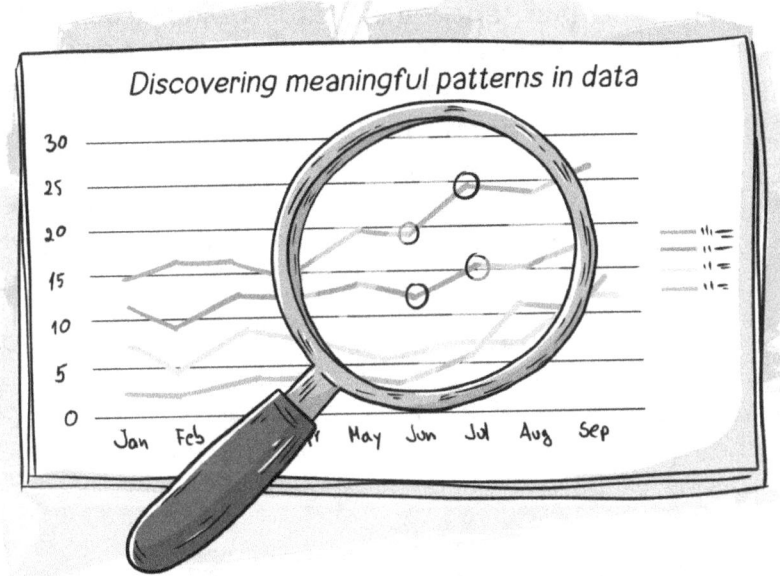

Discovering meaningful patterns in data

Patterns are everywhere — if you know where to look. Spotting patterns and trends in data can help you uncover recurring issues, predict outcomes, and identify hidden opportunities. When you understand these underlying rhythms, you can solve problems proactively instead of reacting to them.

How to Find Patterns and Trends

1. **Collect Data Over Time**

   Patterns often emerge only when you look at information over a period of days, weeks, or months. For example, tracking sales daily might reveal seasonal peaks and dips.

2. **Compare Across Categories**

   Look for similarities or differences between groups. For instance, which products sell best to younger customers versus older ones?

3. Highlight Outliers

Outliers—data points that deviate from the norm—can reveal important insights. For example, if one marketing campaign outperformed others, study why it succeeded.

4. Use Visual Tools

Graphs, heatmaps, and dashboards make it easier to spot trends. For example, a line graph can show if performance is improving or declining over time.

5. Ask "Why?" to Understand Patterns

Once you identify a pattern, dig deeper to understand the cause. For example, if sales increase on weekends, is it because of foot traffic, promotions, or something else?

A Real-Life Example

An e-commerce company tracked customer behavior and noticed a pattern: most cart abandonments occurred on the payment page. Further analysis revealed that unclear pricing was the issue. Simplifying the checkout process increased conversions.

Exercise

Choose a problem and gather data related to it over time. Look for patterns or outliers, and write down one insight you can act on to improve the situation.

Takeaway

Patterns and trends reveal the hidden story behind the numbers. Spot them, understand them, and use them to solve problems before they grow.

Chapter 24: Use Decision Trees for Clarity

When faced with complex decisions, it's easy to feel overwhelmed by all the options. A decision tree is a simple yet powerful tool that helps you map out choices, predict outcomes, and make informed decisions. It works like a flowchart, guiding you through a series of steps and clarifying the consequences of each choice.

Decision trees take the guesswork out of decision-making by helping you visualize your options and their potential outcomes. They're especially helpful for problems that involve multiple paths or uncertain results.

How to Use a Decision Tree

1. **Start with Your Main Question**

   Write the problem or decision at the top of the tree. For example, "Should I expand my business to a new location?"

2. **List Key Choices**

   Identify the main options available to you. For example, "Yes" or "No" to expanding. These form the first branches of the tree.

3. **Add Consequences for Each Choice**

   For every option, map out what could happen next. For example:

   - *If Yes:* Increased revenue, but higher expenses.
   - *If No:* No growth, but stable finances.

4. **Factor in Probabilities and Risks**

   If possible, estimate the likelihood of each outcome. For example, "There's a 70% chance the new location will succeed."

5. **Analyze the Tree**

   Follow each branch to its conclusion. Which path leads to the most desirable outcome based on your goals?

A Real-Life Example

A non-profit deciding whether to launch a new program used a decision tree. They mapped out two paths: launching (with higher costs but greater impact) and not launching (saving money but missing opportunities). By analyzing the potential outcomes, they chose to pilot the program on a small scale first—a decision that balanced risk and reward.

Exercise

Take a decision you're facing. Draw a decision tree, starting with your question at the top. Map out at least two options and the potential consequences of each. Use this visual tool to clarify your next steps.

Takeaway

Decision trees break down complex problems into clear, logical steps. Use them to map choices, predict outcomes, and make smarter decisions.

Chapter 25: Apply Pareto's Principle (80/20 Rule)

Pareto's Principle, also known as the 80/20 Rule, states that 80% of outcomes often come from 20% of inputs. This idea is powerful for problem-solving because it helps you focus your time and energy on the few things that matter most.

Whether you're managing a team, solving a recurring issue, or improving your own productivity, the 80/20 Rule can guide you to prioritize high-impact actions and ignore distractions.

How to Apply the 80/20 Rule

1. **Identify Your Key Inputs**

   Ask, "What are the 20% of actions or resources driving 80% of my results?" For example, in sales, this might mean focusing on your top-performing products or clients.

2. **Eliminate Low-Value Efforts**

   Look for tasks, processes, or habits that consume time but deliver little value. Cutting these frees up energy for more impactful actions.

3. **Focus on High-Impact Activities**

   Spend more time on the things that create the biggest results. For example, if outreach emails bring in most of your clients, prioritize that over less effective strategies.

4. **Reassess Regularly**

   The 80/20 balance isn't fixed. Regularly evaluate what's driving success and adjust your focus accordingly.

5. **Apply It Beyond Work**

   The 80/20 Rule works in all areas of life. For example, 20% of your social interactions may bring you 80% of your happiness. Use this insight to invest more time in what truly matters.

A Real-Life Example

A small business owner discovered that 80% of their revenue came from just 20% of their products. By focusing on promoting and improving those products, they doubled their profits while spending less on less successful items.

Exercise

Look at a project or problem you're working on. Identify the 20% of actions, people, or tools that are driving 80% of the results. Write down how you can focus more on these high-impact areas.

Takeaway

Most results come from a few key efforts. Focus on the 20% that matters, and you'll multiply your impact with less effort.

Chapter 26: Test Your Hypothesis

When solving problems, it's easy to jump to conclusions about what will work. But assumptions can lead you astray. Hypothesis testing is about treating your ideas like experiments: test them, gather results, and refine your approach based on evidence.

This process prevents wasted time and ensures you're solving the real problem with the best solution.

How to Test Your Hypothesis

1. **Define Your Hypothesis**

   Write a clear statement about what you believe to be true. For example, "If we shorten delivery times, customer satisfaction will increase."

2. **Create a Testable Experiment**

   Design a small, manageable test to validate your hypothesis. For example, reduce delivery times for a small group of customers and measure their feedback.

3. **Gather Data**

   Collect evidence from your experiment. Focus on measurable results, like customer satisfaction ratings or sales figures.

4. **Analyze the Results**

   Did the data support your hypothesis? If not, look for clues about what didn't work and adjust your approach.

5. **Refine and Retest**

   Testing is an iterative process. Use your findings to improve your solution and test again if needed.

A Real-Life Example

An app developer hypothesized that simplifying the user interface would increase engagement. They tested this by launching a cleaner design for 10% of users. When engagement jumped by 15%, they rolled out the update to all users with confidence.

Exercise

Think of a problem or idea you're working on. Write a hypothesis about what you think will work, then design a small experiment to test it. Gather results and use them to refine your approach.

Takeaway

Testing your hypothesis turns assumptions into evidence. Experiment, learn, and refine to solve problems with confidence.

Chapter 27: Use Comparative Analysis

When solving a problem, you're often faced with multiple options. How do you decide which one is best? Comparative analysis helps you systematically evaluate choices by weighing their pros, cons, and trade-offs. This method takes the guesswork out of decision-making and ensures you're choosing the most effective path.

Comparative analysis doesn't require complex tools—it's about breaking options down into clear criteria and evaluating them side by side.

How to Use Comparative Analysis

1. **Define Your Criteria**

   Decide what factors matter most for your decision. For example, when choosing a new supplier, you might prioritize cost, reliability, and delivery speed.

2. **List Your Options**

   Write down all the choices you're considering. For example, three potential suppliers.

3. **Score Each Option**

   Rate each option against your criteria on a scale (e.g., 1–10). For example:

   - Supplier A: Cost (8), Reliability (6), Delivery Speed (7).
   - Supplier B: Cost (5), Reliability (9), Delivery Speed (8).

4. **Weigh the Results**

   Add up the scores or use a weighted system if some criteria matter more than others.

5. **Consider Intangibles**

   Numbers don't tell the whole story. Think about qualitative factors, like relationships or brand reputation, that might influence your decision.

A Real-Life Example

A family deciding where to move compared three cities based on job opportunities, cost of living, and school quality. By scoring each city against these criteria, they made an informed choice that balanced practical needs and personal preferences.

Exercise

Pick a decision you're currently facing. Create a table with your options and criteria, then rate each option. Use the results to guide your choice.

Takeaway

Comparative analysis helps you choose wisely by breaking decisions into measurable parts. Weigh your options, and let the data guide you.

Chapter 28: Correlation vs. Causation

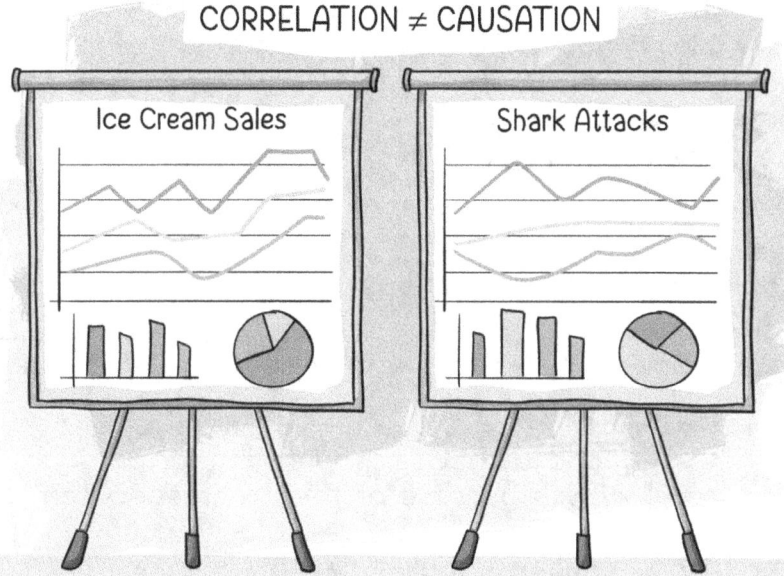

CORRELATION ≠ CAUSATION

Ice Cream Sales

Shark Attacks

Sometimes, two things seem linked because they move together, but that doesn't mean one causes the other. This is the difference between correlation (a relationship) and causation (one thing directly affecting another). Confusing the two can lead to faulty conclusions and wasted efforts.

For example, imagine a city sees more ice cream sales and shark attacks in summer. The correlation is clear, but one doesn't cause the other—they're both tied to the weather.

Understanding this distinction helps you avoid chasing false solutions.

How to Distinguish Correlation from Causation

1. **Look for Timing**

   If A happens before B every time, it could suggest causation. But if they happen simultaneously, it might just be correlation.

2. Consider Other Variables

Ask, "Is there a third factor influencing both?" For example, rising temperatures explain both ice cream sales and shark attacks.

3. Run Experiments

Test whether changing one variable affects the other. For example, if you believe faster customer response times improve satisfaction, try reducing response times and measuring the effect.

4. Avoid Overgeneralizing

Just because two things are linked in one scenario doesn't mean they're always related.

5. Look for Logical Connections

Ask yourself, "Does it make sense that A causes B?" If the connection feels weak or forced, it's likely just correlation.

A Real-Life Example

A company noticed that sales were higher on sunny days and assumed it was because of their marketing campaigns. Further analysis revealed the real cause: better weather increased foot traffic near their store, not their ads.

Exercise

Think of a recent situation where you noticed two trends. Write down possible third factors or alternative explanations to test whether it's correlation or causation.

Takeaway

Correlation doesn't always mean causation. Dig deeper to avoid chasing false connections and focus on real solutions.

Chapter 29: Solve for Variables

In problem-solving, unknowns can feel like roadblocks. Solving for variables means isolating those unknowns, understanding their role, and finding solutions step by step. This structured, logical approach turns complex challenges into manageable puzzles.

Think of it like solving a math problem: instead of trying to tackle everything at once, you focus on the unknown variable and work backward.

How to Solve for Variables

1. **Define the Variables**

   List the unknowns in your problem. For example, "What's causing delays in our production process?"

2. **Break Down the Problem**

   Simplify the problem into smaller parts. For example: delays could be caused by staffing, equipment, or workflow.

3. Test Each Variable

Isolate one variable at a time to test its impact. For example, adjust staffing levels and see if delays improve.

4. Eliminate Non-Factors

Cross off variables that don't affect the outcome. Focus only on the ones that matter.

5. Combine Findings

Once you understand each variable's role, create a plan that addresses them together for a comprehensive solution.

A Real-Life Example

An online store struggling with cart abandonment broke the problem into variables: pricing, shipping speed, and website design. By testing each one, they discovered that unclear pricing was the main issue. Solving this variable reduced cart abandonment by 25%.

Exercise

Write down a problem with multiple unknowns. List the possible variables, test each one's impact, and eliminate those that don't matter.

Takeaway

Solving for variables simplifies complex problems. Isolate the unknowns, test them, and build solutions step by step.

Chapter 30: Simplify the Math

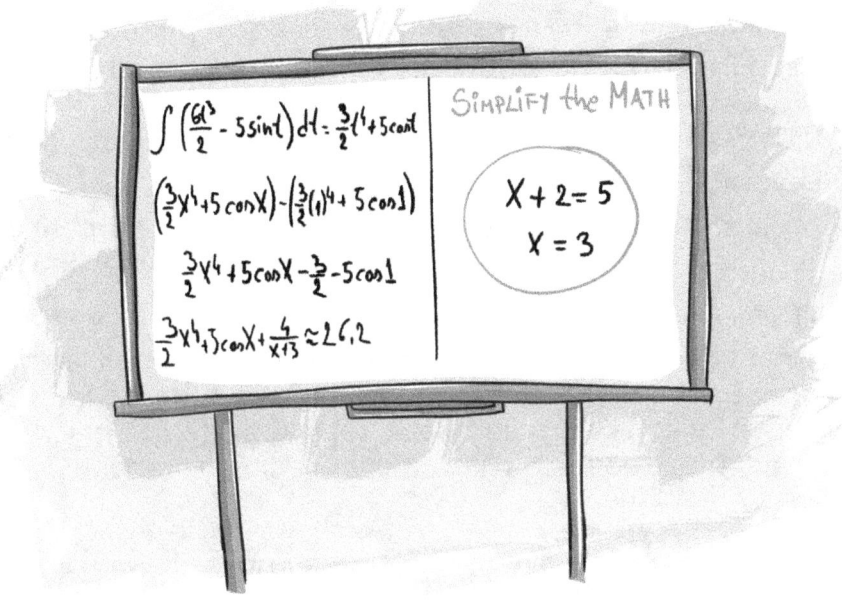

Numbers can feel intimidating, but they're often the key to understanding problems. Simplifying the math means breaking complex calculations into smaller, manageable parts. It's not about being a math genius — it's about making numbers work for you.

From budgets to time estimates, simplifying the math gives you clarity and confidence to make better decisions.

How to Simplify the Math

1. **Focus on the Big Picture**

   Start with rough estimates instead of exact numbers. For example, if a project will take 3–5 weeks, assume 4 weeks and refine as needed.

2. **Break Problems into Steps**

   Divide complex calculations into smaller pieces. For example, if calculating costs for an event, break it into categories like venue, catering, and decorations.

3. Round Numbers When Possible

Use simple estimates instead of precise figures unless accuracy is critical.

4. Use Ratios and Percentages

Ratios can quickly show relationships. For example, "This product accounts for 60% of our revenue" simplifies understanding its importance.

5. Leverage Tools

Use calculators, spreadsheets, or apps to handle repetitive or complex calculations, freeing up mental energy for analysis.

A Real-Life Example

A manager estimating team workloads used simplified math: dividing total hours by team members to determine individual capacity. By rounding numbers, they quickly identified who could handle extra tasks without overloading anyone.

Exercise

Take a problem involving numbers. Simplify it by estimating, rounding, or breaking it into smaller calculations. Reflect on how this makes the problem easier to handle.

Takeaway

Math doesn't have to be complicated. Simplify numbers into manageable steps to gain clarity and confidence in your decisions.

Section 4: Strategic Approaches

Strategy is the bridge between where you are and where you want to go. It's about thinking ahead, weighing trade-offs, and finding the smartest path to success. In this section, you'll learn techniques to plan backward, identify leverage points, and prepare for uncertainty — all while staying focused on what truly matters.

Chapter 31: Plan Backward from Success

One of the best ways to solve a problem is to start at the end. Imagine your goal is already achieved, and then work backward to figure out the steps that got you there. This method, called backward planning, helps you clarify the exact actions you need to take while avoiding unnecessary detours.

Backward planning works because it forces you to think about the big picture. Instead of asking, "What do I do next?" you're asking, "What needs to happen to achieve the outcome I want?"

How to Plan Backward

1. **Visualize the Goal**

   Imagine your goal is already accomplished. What does success look like? Be as specific as possible. For example: "I've successfully launched my online store with 20 products available."

2. **Identify the Last Step**

What's the final action required to reach the goal? For example, "Launch the website."

3. **Work Backward, Step by Step**

Trace the path in reverse, identifying each necessary step. For example:

- o   Test the website.
- o   Upload product photos and descriptions.
- o   Set up payment systems.

4. **Refine and Organize**

Rearrange the steps into a logical order and identify dependencies (e.g., you can't upload product photos until they're taken).

5. **Create a Timeline**

Assign deadlines to each step to ensure you stay on track.

A Real-Life Example

An event planner organizing a conference started by imagining the final day of the event: attendees leaving satisfied with the experience. Working backward, they identified steps like confirming speakers, booking the venue, and promoting the event. This backward plan ensured nothing important was missed.

Exercise

Think of a current goal. Write down the end result, then work backward to identify at least five steps needed to achieve it. Rearrange them into a timeline and start with the first step.

Takeaway

Planning backward from success gives you a clear roadmap to achieve your goals. Start at the finish line and trace the path step by step.

Chapter 32: Think Like a Chess Player

Great problem-solving requires thinking several steps ahead, just like in chess. Chess players don't focus only on their next move—they consider how each action affects future moves and anticipate what their opponent might do in response.

By thinking strategically, you can anticipate obstacles, plan countermeasures, and create solutions that hold up over time.

How to Think Like a Chess Player

1. **Look Beyond the Immediate Problem**

   Ask, "What happens after I solve this?" For example, if you cut costs to boost profits, will quality suffer and drive customers away?

2. **Consider Multiple Scenarios**

   Think about how your actions might play out in different ways. What's the best-case, worst-case, and most likely outcome?

3. Anticipate Challenges

Identify potential obstacles and plan how you'll address them. For example, if a competitor responds to your new product, how will you maintain your edge?

4. Think in Chains of Events

Visualize how one decision leads to another. For example:

- o Hire more staff → Faster production → Higher customer satisfaction → Increased revenue.

5. Adapt as the Game Changes

Be ready to adjust your strategy based on new information or unexpected developments.

A Real-Life Example

A tech start-up planning to launch a new app anticipated that competitors would try to copy their features. They thought ahead by securing patents and creating unique branding, ensuring long-term success even if others entered the market.

Exercise

Think about a problem you're solving. Write down how your solution could affect future events. Identify one potential challenge and plan a countermeasure.

Takeaway

Strategic problem-solving means thinking several steps ahead. Anticipate challenges and consider the ripple effects of your decisions.

Chapter 33: Leverage Opportunity Costs

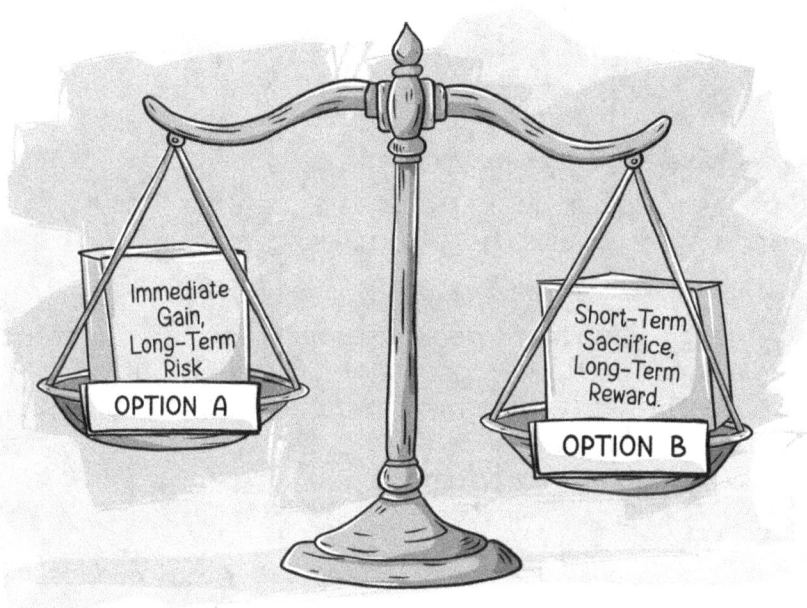

Every decision you make has a cost — what you give up by choosing one option over another. This is called opportunity cost. By understanding and weighing these trade-offs, you can make smarter decisions that maximize value and minimize regret.

How to Weigh Opportunity Costs

1. **Identify What You're Giving Up**

   For every choice, ask, "What am I missing out on by choosing this?" For example, if you spend $1,000 on advertising, you can't use that money for product development.

2. **Quantify the Trade-Offs**

   Estimate the potential value of each option. Which one offers the biggest payoff?

3. **Think Long-Term**

   Opportunity costs aren't always immediate. For example, skipping an investment in training today could lead to lost productivity down the line.

4. **Consider Hidden Costs**

   Some costs aren't obvious at first. For example, choosing a cheap supplier might save money upfront but lead to quality issues later.

5. **Prioritize High-Value Options**

   Focus on decisions that offer the greatest long-term value, even if they require short-term sacrifices.

A Real-Life Example

A college student deciding between two internships considered opportunity costs. One paid well but offered little growth potential, while the other had no pay but provided valuable experience. Choosing the second internship led to a high-paying job after graduation.

Exercise

Think about a decision you're facing. Write down what you'll gain and lose from each option. Compare the long-term value of each choice and prioritize accordingly.

Takeaway

Every choice has a cost. Weigh the trade-offs and focus on decisions that maximize value over the long term.

Chapter 34: Identify Key Leverage Points

Not all actions are created equal. Some have an outsized impact, like flipping the right switch in a complex system. These are leverage points—small changes that lead to significant results. By identifying and focusing on leverage points, you can solve problems more efficiently and effectively.

How to Find Leverage Points

1. **Map the Problem**

   Break the problem into its components and look for areas where small adjustments could ripple outward.

2. **Focus on Bottlenecks**

   Identify the one factor slowing everything down. Fixing this can improve the entire process.

3. **Look for High-Impact Actions**

   Ask, "Which change will produce the biggest result?" For example, improving team communication could reduce delays across multiple projects.

4. Test Small Changes

Experiment with minor adjustments to see how they affect the system as a whole.

5. Refine and Scale

Once you've identified a successful leverage point, focus your resources there for maximum impact.

A Real-Life Example

A factory struggling with slow production found that a single bottleneck—an outdated machine — was causing delays. Upgrading the machine improved efficiency across the entire assembly line.

Exercise

Write down the components of a current problem. Identify one area where a small change could create a big impact. Test it and measure the results.

Takeaway

Leverage points are where small changes create big results. Identify them, focus your efforts, and amplify your impact.

Chapter 35: Map the System (Systems Thinking)

Problems rarely exist in isolation. They're part of larger systems where actions in one area ripple out and affect others. Systems thinking helps you see the big picture by mapping out how all the parts of a problem interact. Instead of treating symptoms, you can address the system as a whole, finding solutions that work long-term.

How to Use Systems Thinking

1. **Identify the System**

   Define the system you're working with. Is it a team, a business process, or a community issue?

2. **List the Components**

   Break the system into its key parts. For example, in a supply chain, components might include suppliers, transportation, and storage.

3. Trace Interconnections

Map how each component influences others. For example, delays in transportation might disrupt storage, which affects customer satisfaction.

4. Look for Feedback Loops

Feedback loops occur when actions reinforce or counteract one another. For example, positive feedback loops (like word-of-mouth marketing) amplify success, while negative loops (like repeated mistakes) perpetuate failure.

5. Address Root Causes, Not Symptoms

Use your system map to find where the problem originates. Fixing one part of the system often improves everything else.

A Real-Life Example

A school struggling with low student performance used systems thinking to map the problem. They discovered that a lack of teacher training (one component) was affecting classroom engagement, leading to lower test scores. By improving teacher training, they strengthened the entire system.

Exercise

Choose a problem and list its components. Draw a simple map showing how the parts are connected. Identify one area where a small change could positively affect the whole system.

Takeaway

Every problem exists within a system. Map out the parts, find the connections, and solve for the whole, not just the symptoms.

Chapter 36: Scenario Planning for Uncertainty

The future is uncertain, but that doesn't mean you have to feel unprepared. Scenario planning is a strategic tool that helps you anticipate multiple possible outcomes and prepare for them. By imagining "what if" scenarios, you can adapt to surprises, seize opportunities, and minimize risks.

How to Use Scenario Planning

1. **Define the Decision or Problem**

   Start with a specific challenge, like launching a new product or responding to market changes.

2. **Identify Key Variables**

   List factors that could influence the outcome, such as customer demand, economic conditions, or competitor actions.

3. Create Scenarios

Develop three scenarios:

- o Best case: Everything goes better than expected.
- o Worst case: Major obstacles arise.
- o Most likely case: A realistic middle ground.

4. Plan for Each Scenario

Outline how you'd respond to each outcome. For example, if demand spikes (best case), you might need extra inventory; if demand drops (worst case), you might adjust your marketing strategy.

5. Stay Flexible

Scenario planning isn't about predicting the future—it's about staying adaptable no matter what happens.

A Real-Life Example

An event organizer used scenario planning for an outdoor concert. They prepared for sunny weather (best case), rain (worst case), and cloudy skies (most likely). When rain arrived, they smoothly implemented their backup plan, minimizing disruptions.

Exercise

Choose a decision or challenge. Write down three possible scenarios (best, worst, most likely) and one action you could take for each.

Takeaway

Scenario planning helps you navigate uncertainty with confidence. Prepare for the best, worst, and everything in between.

Chapter 37: Build in Redundancy

Redundancy isn't wasteful—it's essential for reducing risks and improving resilience. Whether it's backup systems, extra resources, or contingency plans, redundancy ensures that if one part fails, you're not left scrambling.

Think of it like carrying a spare tire: you might never need it, but when you do, it saves the day.

How to Build in Redundancy

1. **Identify Critical Areas**

   Focus on the parts of your plan or system where failure would cause the most damage.

2. **Create Backups**

   Build duplicate systems or resources. For example, keep extra supplies on hand or train multiple team members for key roles.

3. **Distribute Responsibilities**

   Avoid relying on a single person or system. Spreading tasks across multiple people reduces the risk of disruption.

4. Test Your Redundancies

Regularly check your backups to ensure they're functional. For example, test emergency procedures or backup servers.

5. Balance Costs with Benefits

Redundancy comes with costs, so prioritize critical areas where the potential payoff is worth the investment.

A Real-Life Example

Airlines build redundancy into their operations with backup pilots, extra fuel reserves, and duplicate navigation systems. These measures ensure passenger safety even when unexpected issues arise.

Exercise

Think of a project or system you rely on. Identify one critical area and create a simple backup or redundancy plan to protect against failure.

Takeaway

Redundancy is your safety net. Build backups and contingency plans to reduce risks and stay prepared for the unexpected.

Chapter 38: Focus on Long-Term Impact

Some solutions provide quick wins but don't last, while others take time to implement but deliver lasting value. Focusing on long-term impact means prioritizing decisions that create sustainable results, even if they require patience.

How to Focus on Long-Term Impact

1. **Define Your Big Picture Goals**

   Ask, "What outcome do I want in 1, 5, or 10 years?" Let this guide your decision-making.

2. **Weigh Short-Term vs. Long-Term Benefits**

   Avoid sacrificing long-term gains for quick fixes. For example, cutting staff might save money now but harm productivity later.

3. **Invest in Foundational Changes**

   Focus on solutions that strengthen the core of your system, such as improving skills, processes, or infrastructure.

4. Be Patient with Results

Long-term solutions often take time to show their impact. Stay committed and track progress over time.

5. Regularly Reassess

Periodically evaluate whether your efforts are still aligned with your long-term goals.

A Real-Life Example

A company struggling with high turnover invested in employee training and career development programs. While costly upfront, this strategy reduced turnover and boosted morale, creating a stronger workforce over time.

Exercise

Think of a current challenge. Write down one short-term solution and one long-term solution. Compare their impact and prioritize the option that delivers sustainable results.

Takeaway

Long-term thinking creates lasting success. Prioritize decisions that build sustainable value over time.

Chapter 39: Prioritize Quick Wins

Sometimes, the best way to solve a big problem is to start small. Quick wins are easy, high-impact solutions that build momentum and boost confidence. By tackling these first, you can create a ripple effect that drives progress toward bigger goals.

How to Prioritize Quick Wins

1. **Look for Low-Hanging Fruit**

   Identify solutions that are simple to implement but have noticeable benefits.

2. **Focus on High-Impact Areas**

   Choose wins that address key pain points or create visible improvements.

3. **Use Wins to Build Momentum**

   Success inspires further action. Use early wins to motivate your team or keep yourself moving forward.

4. **Balance Wins with Long-Term Goals**

   Quick wins are important, but don't let them distract from larger objectives.

5. **Celebrate Success**

   Acknowledge and reward progress to maintain energy and focus.

A Real-Life Example

A project manager turned around a struggling team by starting with small, achievable goals, like improving meeting efficiency. These quick wins boosted morale and created momentum for tackling larger challenges.

Exercise

Think of a problem you're facing. Identify one quick win—an action you can complete in a day or two—that would create positive momentum. Take that action today.

Takeaway

Quick wins build confidence and momentum. Start small to create a ripple effect that drives big results.

Chapter 40: Think Incrementally

Big problems don't have to be solved all at once. Incremental thinking means breaking solutions into smaller, manageable steps and tackling them one at a time. This approach makes even the most daunting challenges feel achievable.

How to Think Incrementally

1. **Break the Problem Into Stages**

   Divide the challenge into logical phases. For example, "Research," "Plan," "Execute."

2. **Set Milestones**

   Define clear, measurable checkpoints along the way to track progress.

3. **Focus on the Next Step**

   Avoid getting overwhelmed by the big picture. Concentrate on completing one step at a time.

4. **Iterate and Improve**

   Treat each step as a chance to learn and refine your approach.

5. **Celebrate Progress**

   Acknowledge small wins at every milestone to stay motivated.

A Real-Life Example

An author writing a novel broke the process into daily word count goals. By focusing on writing 500 words a day, they completed the entire book in six months without feeling overwhelmed.

Exercise

Choose a big goal and break it into three stages. Focus on completing just the first step this week and celebrate your progress.

Takeaway

Incremental progress turns big problems into manageable steps. Solve one stage at a time and build your way to success.

Section 5: Collaborative Problem-Solving

Some problems are too big or complex to solve alone. Collaborative problem-solving taps into the power of teamwork, bringing together diverse skills, perspectives, and ideas to create better solutions. In this section, you'll learn how to listen effectively, build consensus, and avoid common pitfalls like groupthink—all while strengthening your team's ability to solve problems together.

Chapter 41: Harness the Power of Teamwork

They say "two heads are better than one," but why stop at two? Teamwork accelerates problem-solving by combining different skills, knowledge, and perspectives. A well-coordinated team can accomplish more than any individual because they pool strengths, share responsibilities, and support each other through challenges.

However, teamwork isn't just about gathering people — it's about coordinating efforts and fostering collaboration.

How to Harness the Power of Teamwork

1. **Clarify Roles and Goals**

   Make sure everyone knows their role and the ultimate goal. Ambiguity leads to confusion and duplication of effort.

2. **Leverage Individual Strengths**

   Assign tasks based on each person's unique skills. For example, one team member might excel at data analysis, while another shines in creative brainstorming.

3. **Encourage Open Communication**

   Foster an environment where team members feel comfortable sharing ideas and feedback.

4. **Coordinate Efforts**

   Use tools like project management software or regular check-ins to keep everyone aligned and on track.

5. **Celebrate Team Wins**

   Recognize and reward the team's collective achievements to maintain motivation and morale.

A Real-Life Example

A start-up facing tight deadlines divided tasks among team members based on their expertise. Designers focused on visuals, developers handled functionality, and marketers crafted messaging. By working in sync, they launched their product on time and exceeded expectations.

Exercise

Think of a challenge that would benefit from teamwork. Write down each person's potential role and how their skills contribute to the solution. Then, create a plan to collaborate effectively.

Takeaway

Teamwork solves problems faster and smarter. Combine strengths, coordinate efforts, and watch your team achieve more together.

Chapter 42: Listen Before Solving

It's tempting to jump straight into solutions, especially when faced with a problem. But the best solutions come from fully understanding the issue—and that requires listening first. Listening uncovers key details, builds trust, and ensures that everyone feels heard, which is critical for effective collaboration.

How to Listen Before Solving

1. **Ask Open-Ended Questions**

   Encourage people to share their thoughts by asking questions like, "What do you think is causing this problem?" or "How do you think we should address it?"

2. **Avoid Interrupting**

   Let others finish speaking before jumping in. Interruptions can shut down valuable insights.

3. **Clarify and Summarize**

   Repeat back what you've heard to confirm your understanding. For example: "So you're saying the delays are due to unclear instructions?"

4. **Pay Attention to Non-Verbal Cues**

   Body language and tone often reveal more than words alone.

5. **Hold Off on Judgments**

   Stay open to all perspectives, even if they differ from your initial assumptions.

A Real-Life Example

A manager dealing with low team morale started by holding one-on-one listening sessions with employees. They discovered that unclear goals and a lack of recognition were key issues. By addressing these concerns, morale improved dramatically.

Exercise

In your next team discussion, focus on listening. Ask open-ended questions, summarize what you hear, and avoid interrupting. Reflect on how this changes the conversation.

Takeaway

Listening uncovers the heart of the problem. Understand first, then solve—it's the fastest path to meaningful solutions.

Chapter 43: Balance Diverse Perspectives

Diversity is a superpower in problem-solving. Different perspectives—shaped by backgrounds, skills, or experiences—reveal insights and ideas that a single viewpoint might miss. But balancing those perspectives takes skill, especially when opinions conflict.

By valuing and integrating diverse viewpoints, you create richer solutions that work for everyone involved.

How to Balance Diverse Perspectives

1. **Create a Safe Space for Sharing**

   Encourage all team members to voice their opinions without fear of judgment.

2. **Actively Seek Out Differences**

   Ask, "What's another way to look at this?" or "Does anyone see a risk we're missing?"

3. **Bridge Conflicting Views**

   Look for common ground or compromises between opposing ideas. For example, one person's push for speed might align with another's focus on quality through better planning.

4. **Use a Mediator if Needed**

   When disagreements escalate, a neutral party can help ensure every voice is heard.

5. **Synthesize Ideas**

   Combine elements from different perspectives to create a stronger, more inclusive solution.

A Real-Life Example

A non-profit solving a community issue invited input from residents, local businesses, and government officials. By balancing their diverse priorities, they created a solution that satisfied all parties and gained widespread support.

Exercise

Think of a decision where multiple perspectives could help. Gather input from at least three people with different viewpoints and combine their ideas into a single, balanced solution.

Takeaway

Diverse perspectives strengthen problem-solving. Seek out differences, bridge gaps, and build solutions that reflect the whole picture.

Chapter 44: Build Consensus with Stakeholders

Great solutions only work if everyone involved is on board. Building consensus means aligning stakeholders—team members, leaders, customers, or partners—around a shared goal. While it takes effort, consensus smooths implementation and ensures lasting results.

How to Build Consensus

1. **Identify Stakeholders**

   List everyone affected by the decision. For example, employees, clients, or external partners.

2. **Communicate Early and Often**

   Share the problem, potential solutions, and progress updates. Transparent communication builds trust.

3. **Address Concerns**

   Listen to objections and adjust your approach if needed. Consensus doesn't mean forcing agreement—it means finding a solution everyone can support.

4. **Highlight Shared Goals**

   Focus on common objectives to unite stakeholders. For example, "We all want this project to succeed."

5. **Confirm Commitment**

   Before moving forward, ensure that everyone is aligned and committed to the plan.

A Real-Life Example

A company rolling out a new policy gained consensus by holding feedback sessions with employees and management. By addressing concerns early, they avoided resistance and ensured smooth implementation.

Exercise

Choose a project or problem involving multiple stakeholders. Hold a meeting to share updates, gather feedback, and address concerns. Focus on aligning everyone toward a shared goal.

Takeaway

Consensus builds trust and ensures smoother implementation. Align stakeholders early to create solutions that work for everyone.

Chapter 45: Use Structured Decision-Making

Group decisions can easily become chaotic without structure. Structured decision-making provides a clear, step-by-step process for evaluating options and reaching a conclusion. This approach minimizes bias, ensures fairness, and keeps the team focused.

How to Use Structured Decision-Making

1. **Define the Problem Clearly**

   Make sure everyone understands the issue. For example, "How should we allocate next year's budget?"

2. **Set Criteria for Evaluation**

   Agree on the factors that will guide the decision, like cost, time, or impact.

3. **Generate and Compare Options**

   Brainstorm solutions, then evaluate each one against the criteria.

4. Vote or Decide by Consensus

Use tools like majority voting, weighted scoring, or consensus-building to finalize the choice.

5. Document the Decision

Record the reasoning behind the choice to avoid confusion later.

A Real-Life Example

A school district deciding on a new curriculum used structured decision-making. They listed key criteria (student outcomes, cost, teacher training) and scored each option. This transparent process gained widespread support.

Exercise

Think of a group decision you need to make. Set criteria, list options, and use a structured method (like weighted scoring) to choose the best solution.

Takeaway

Structured decision-making brings clarity and fairness to group choices. Follow a clear process for smarter, more efficient decisions.

Chapter 46: Avoid Groupthink

Groupthink is the enemy of smart collaboration. It happens when team members prioritize harmony and agreement over critical thinking and honest debate. While it may feel easier to agree quickly, groupthink often leads to poor decisions because key perspectives are ignored, and potential risks are overlooked.

Avoiding groupthink doesn't mean fostering endless conflict—it means creating a culture where questioning and disagreement are welcomed. When people feel safe to challenge ideas, the team produces stronger, more creative solutions.

How to Avoid Groupthink

1. **Encourage Dissent**

   Let your team know it's okay to challenge ideas. Ask directly, "Does anyone see risks or flaws in this plan?" This invites constructive feedback.

2. **Assign a Devil's Advocate**

   Designate someone to intentionally poke holes in the group's ideas. This forces the team to consider alternative perspectives.

3. **Welcome Diverse Opinions**

   Bring in people with different expertise, backgrounds, or experiences. Diversity naturally challenges groupthink by introducing new viewpoints.

4. **Separate Idea Generation from Evaluation**

   During brainstorming, focus on gathering ideas without judgment. Once you've collected them, evaluate critically to identify the strongest options.

5. **Use Anonymous Feedback**

   If group dynamics make people hesitant to speak up, use tools like anonymous surveys or suggestion boxes to gather honest opinions.

A Real-Life Example

In 1961, the U.S. Bay of Pigs invasion failed partly due to groupthink. Leaders didn't challenge the plan, even though flaws were clear. NASA learned from this and implemented dissent-focused practices for future missions, improving decision-making and avoiding disasters like the Challenger launch.

Exercise

Think of a recent group decision. Ask yourself: Was dissent encouraged, or did the group rush to agreement? Write down one way you could create space for critical feedback in future discussions.

Takeaway

Groupthink weakens decision-making. Foster a culture of respectful dissent and critical thinking to create stronger, more innovative solutions.

Chapter 47: Delegate and Share Responsibility

When solving complex problems, trying to do everything yourself isn't just exhausting—it's inefficient. Delegation allows you to distribute tasks strategically, leveraging the strengths of each team member and speeding up progress. Sharing responsibility also empowers others, builds trust, and ensures that no single person is overloaded.

The key to effective delegation is clarity: knowing who's doing what, why, and how it fits into the bigger picture.

How to Delegate and Share Responsibility

1. Match Tasks to Strengths

Assign tasks based on each person's skills and expertise. For example, a detail-oriented team member might handle scheduling, while a creative thinker works on brainstorming.

2. **Be Clear About Expectations**

   Outline exactly what needs to be done, why it matters, and the timeline for completion. Ambiguity leads to missed deadlines and frustration.

3. **Provide the Right Resources**

   Make sure everyone has the tools, information, and support they need to succeed.

4. **Empower, Don't Micromanage**

   Trust your team to handle their responsibilities. Check in for updates, but avoid hovering over every detail.

5. **Hold Everyone Accountable**

   Regularly review progress and celebrate milestones. If something goes off track, address it constructively and collaboratively.

A Real-Life Example

A marketing manager overwhelmed by a product launch delegated tasks like social media campaigns, graphic design, and analytics tracking to her team. By trusting their skills and providing clear guidance, the team delivered a successful campaign on time, freeing the manager to focus on strategy.

Exercise

Think of a project where you're taking on too much. Identify one task you can delegate to someone better suited for it. Write down clear instructions and provide the necessary resources to set them up for success.

Takeaway

Delegation isn't about offloading work—it's about sharing responsibility strategically. Leverage your team's strengths to achieve more, faster.

Chapter 48: Seek External Expertise

Sometimes, solving a problem requires knowledge or skills beyond your team's expertise. Bringing in an external expert—whether a consultant, specialist, or experienced mentor—can provide fresh insights and save you from costly mistakes.

Experts don't just bring knowledge; they offer perspective. They can spot blind spots, propose strategies you hadn't considered, and help you navigate challenges more efficiently.

How to Seek External Expertise

1. **Identify Knowledge Gaps**

   Be honest about what your team doesn't know or lacks experience in. For example, you might need help with legal issues, technical development, or customer research.

2. **Find the Right Expert**

   Look for someone with proven experience in the specific area. This could be a consultant, an industry leader, or even a colleague with niche expertise.

3. Collaborate, Don't Abdicate

Use the expert's guidance to inform your decisions, but stay involved. Experts enhance your process—they don't replace it.

4. Ask Targeted Questions

Come prepared with clear, specific questions to maximize the value of the expert's input.

5. Integrate Their Insights

Once you've gathered their advice, work with your team to adapt it to your unique context.

A Real-Life Example

When a small business faced a cybersecurity breach, they hired a cybersecurity expert to assess vulnerabilities and implement protections. The expert not only resolved the immediate issue but also trained the team to prevent future attacks.

Exercise

Think about a current challenge. Identify one area where an expert could provide valuable insights. Research potential experts or resources and plan to reach out for help.

Takeaway

You don't have to solve every problem alone. Seek external expertise to fill knowledge gaps, gain fresh perspectives, and navigate challenges more effectively.

Chapter 49: Communicate Solutions Effectively

Even the best solutions fail if they aren't communicated clearly. Whether you're presenting an idea to stakeholders, explaining changes to a team, or persuading a client, effective communication ensures everyone understands and supports the plan.

Clear communication is about more than sharing information—it's about building trust, addressing concerns, and inspiring action.

How to Communicate Solutions Effectively

1. **Know Your Audience**

   Tailor your message to the needs and priorities of the people you're speaking to. What do they care about most?

2. **Keep It Simple**

   Avoid jargon and overly complex explanations. Break the solution into clear, digestible steps.

3. **Use Visuals**

   Charts, diagrams, or slides make complex ideas easier to grasp.

4. **Address Concerns**

   Anticipate questions or objections and address them proactively. For example, explain how risks will be mitigated.

5. **End with a Call to Action**

   Clearly state what you need from your audience, whether it's approval, feedback, or next steps.

A Real-Life Example

A project manager presenting a new workflow to their team used a simple diagram to show how tasks would flow more efficiently. By explaining the benefits clearly and inviting questions, they gained team buy-in and implemented the changes smoothly.

Exercise

Think of a solution you need to communicate. Write a simple outline of your main points, including benefits, steps, and potential concerns. Practice presenting it to ensure clarity.

Takeaway

Clear communication turns ideas into action. Simplify your message, address concerns, and inspire your audience to support your solution.

Chapter 50: Resolve Conflicts Constructively

Conflict is inevitable in collaborative problem-solving, but it doesn't have to derail progress. When managed constructively, disagreements can lead to deeper understanding, stronger relationships, and better solutions.

The goal isn't to avoid conflict — it's to handle it with respect and focus on finding common ground.

How to Resolve Conflicts Constructively

1. **Stay Calm and Objective**

   Emotions can escalate conflicts. Focus on the problem, not the person.

2. **Listen Actively**

   Let everyone involved share their perspective without interruption. Understanding all sides is key to resolution.

3. **Focus on Shared Goals**

   Highlight common objectives to shift the focus from differences to collaboration. For example, "We all want this project to succeed."

4. **Brainstorm Solutions Together**

   Invite all parties to propose solutions. This fosters ownership and reduces resistance.

5. **Document Agreements**

   Once a resolution is reached, write it down to ensure clarity and accountability.

A Real-Life Example

Two departments clashing over resource allocation resolved their conflict by holding a facilitated meeting. By listening to each other's priorities and focusing on shared goals, they created a plan that balanced both teams' needs.

Exercise

Think of a recent conflict you've encountered. Write down the shared goals of everyone involved and one way you could encourage collaboration toward a resolution.

Takeaway

Conflict can lead to growth when handled constructively. Listen, focus on common goals, and work together to find solutions.

Section 6: Emotional Intelligence in Problem-Solving

Problem-solving isn't just about logic and strategy — it's also about understanding and managing emotions. Emotional intelligence helps you stay calm, think clearly, and connect with others during challenges. In this section, you'll learn how to manage stress, cultivate empathy, and build resilience, all while using your emotions as a strength, not a barrier, in solving problems.

Chapter 51: Stay Calm Under Pressure

Stressful situations make it easy to panic, but staying calm under pressure is essential for effective problem-solving. When emotions run high, your brain shifts into fight-or-flight mode, making it harder to think clearly or make rational decisions. Staying calm isn't about ignoring stress — it's about controlling your response to it.

Calmness gives you the clarity and focus to find solutions, no matter how intense the challenge.

How to Stay Calm Under Pressure

1. **Pause and Breathe**

   When stress spikes, take a moment to focus on your breath. Deep, slow breaths signal to your brain that it's safe to relax, helping you regain control.

2. Break the Problem into Steps

Overwhelm fuels panic. Simplify the situation by breaking it into smaller, manageable tasks and tackling them one at a time.

3. Focus on What You Can Control

Stress often comes from worrying about things outside your control. Shift your attention to what you *can* influence.

4. Reframe the Situation

Instead of seeing pressure as a threat, view it as a challenge. This mindset shift boosts confidence and keeps you focused.

5. Practice Calm in Small Moments

Build your resilience by practicing calmness in less stressful situations, like traffic jams or minor setbacks.

A Real-Life Example

During an emergency at a hospital, a nurse stayed calm by focusing on her training and breaking the chaos into clear steps: assessing the patient, calling for help, and stabilizing the situation. Her composure ensured the team acted efficiently, saving a life.

Exercise

Think of a recent stressful situation. Reflect on how you reacted and write down one way you could have stayed calmer. Practice deep breathing the next time stress arises.

Takeaway

Calmness is your superpower in high-pressure moments. Pause, breathe, and focus on what you can control to think clearly and act decisively.

Chapter 52: Recognize Emotional Triggers

Emotions are powerful — they can help or hinder problem-solving, depending on how well you manage them. Emotional triggers are the moments when something causes a strong reaction, like frustration when a plan fails or doubt when someone challenges your idea. Recognizing these triggers helps you pause, reflect, and respond thoughtfully instead of reacting impulsively.

How to Recognize Emotional Triggers

1. **Notice Physical Signs**

   Pay attention to your body's reactions—tight shoulders, a racing heart, or clenched fists often signal emotional triggers.

2. **Identify Patterns**

   Reflect on past situations that triggered strong emotions. What were the common themes or circumstances?

3. Name the Emotion

When you feel triggered, label the emotion: "I'm feeling frustrated." Naming it helps you distance yourself from it and regain control.

4. Pause Before Responding

Take a moment to process your feelings before acting. A short pause can prevent impulsive decisions.

5. Understand the Root Cause

Ask yourself, "Why am I feeling this way?" Often, the trigger stems from deeper fears or insecurities that can be addressed.

A Real-Life Example

A manager who often felt defensive during team feedback realized his trigger was a fear of failure. By recognizing this, he began approaching feedback as a learning opportunity, improving both his leadership and team trust.

Exercise

Write down one situation where you recently felt triggered. What emotion did you experience, and what caused it? Reflect on how you might handle it differently next time.

Takeaway

Recognizing your emotional triggers puts you back in control. Identify patterns, name the emotion, and respond thoughtfully instead of reacting impulsively.

Chapter 53: Reframe Negative Thinking

Negative thinking can trap you in a cycle of doubt and pessimism, making it harder to see solutions. Reframing means shifting your perspective to focus on possibilities instead of problems. It's not about ignoring challenges but about choosing constructive thoughts that drive action.

Reframing turns setbacks into opportunities, making you more adaptable and resilient.

How to Reframe Negative Thinking

1. **Notice Negative Thoughts**

   Pay attention to internal dialogue like, "This will never work" or "I always mess up."

2. **Challenge the Thought**

   Ask yourself, "Is this really true?" Often, negative thinking is based on assumptions, not facts.

3. **Replace "What's Wrong?" with "What's Possible?"**

   Shift your focus to what you can learn or achieve. For example, "What can I do differently next time?"

4. **Focus on Progress, Not Perfection**

   Instead of fixating on what went wrong, celebrate small wins and improvements.

5. **Practice Gratitude**

   Reflect on what's going well or what you've learned from the situation. Gratitude boosts optimism and creativity.

A Real-Life Example

An entrepreneur whose product launch failed reframed the experience as a learning opportunity. Instead of giving up, they used customer feedback to redesign the product, leading to a successful relaunch.

Exercise

Write down one negative thought you've had about a current challenge. Challenge it by asking, "What's one positive thing I can take from this situation?"

Takeaway

Negative thinking clouds judgment. Reframe challenges as opportunities, and you'll unlock constructive action and better solutions.

Chapter 54: Empathy as a Problem-Solving Tool

Empathy — putting yourself in someone else's shoes — is one of the most powerful tools in problem-solving. It allows you to understand the emotions, motivations, and needs behind a problem, leading to solutions that truly work for everyone involved.

Empathy is especially critical in conflicts or customer-facing issues, where understanding the other person's perspective often reveals the root of the problem.

How to Use Empathy in Problem-Solving

1. **Listen Without Judgment**

   Focus on what the other person is saying, not how you want to respond.

2. **Ask Open-Ended Questions**

   Questions like "How do you feel about this?" or "What would make this better for you?" uncover valuable insights.

3. **Imagine Their Perspective**

   Visualize how the problem looks and feels from their viewpoint.

4. **Acknowledge Their Emotions**

   Validate their feelings by saying things like, "I can see why this would be frustrating."

5. **Design Solutions for Their Needs**

   Use what you've learned to create solutions that address their priorities, not just your own.

A Real-Life Example

A customer service team reduced complaints by empathizing with customers. Instead of sticking to scripts, they listened to frustrations, acknowledged emotions, and offered personalized solutions. This approach increased customer satisfaction by 30%.

Exercise

Think of someone impacted by a current problem. Write down what the situation might feel like from their perspective and one way you could address their needs more effectively.

Takeaway

Empathy bridges gaps and uncovers deeper insights. Understand others' perspectives to create solutions that truly work for everyone.

Chapter 55: Manage Stress for Clearer Thinking

Stress is a natural part of problem-solving, but too much of it clouds your thinking and leads to poor decisions. Managing stress doesn't mean eliminating it entirely—it means controlling it so you can stay focused and productive. When you're calm, your brain works better, helping you find creative, effective solutions.

By managing stress, you create the mental clarity and emotional stability needed to approach problems with confidence.

How to Manage Stress for Clearer Thinking

1. Identify Your Stress Triggers

Notice what situations or thoughts cause you stress. Knowing your triggers helps you prepare and respond calmly.

2. **Practice Mindfulness**

   Mindfulness exercises, like focusing on your breath or a single task, help you stay grounded in the present moment.

3. **Prioritize Self-Care**

   Regular exercise, sleep, and healthy eating strengthen your ability to handle stress.

4. **Set Realistic Expectations**

   Avoid overloading yourself. Break tasks into smaller steps, and focus on one thing at a time.

5. **Use Stress as a Signal**

   Instead of fearing stress, treat it as a sign that something needs attention. Use it to motivate action rather than freeze in worry.

A Real-Life Example

A project manager facing tight deadlines felt overwhelmed by a growing to-do list. By taking a 10-minute mindfulness break each morning and organizing tasks into smaller, manageable chunks, she stayed calm and delivered the project successfully.

Exercise

Write down one current stressor. Identify one action you can take to reduce its intensity, whether it's pausing to breathe, delegating tasks, or rethinking your priorities.

Takeaway

Stress is manageable. Stay calm by recognizing your triggers, focusing on self-care, and taking intentional steps to clear your mind.

Chapter 56: Practice Self-Awareness

Great problem-solving starts with understanding yourself. Self-awareness is the ability to recognize your thoughts, emotions, and biases—and how they influence your decisions. Without it, you might misjudge situations or let emotions cloud your judgment.

By practicing self-awareness, you can make decisions based on logic and clarity rather than impulse or habit.

How to Practice Self-Awareness

1. **Identify Your Biases**

   Reflect on your tendencies to favor certain ideas or ignore others. Ask yourself, "Am I being objective?"

2. **Pay Attention to Emotions**

   Notice when emotions like frustration or excitement are driving your decisions. Name them to reduce their power.

3. Reflect on Past Decisions

Think about situations where your assumptions or reactions influenced the outcome. What would you do differently?

4. Ask for Feedback

Others often see things you miss. Ask trusted colleagues or friends how your behavior or decision-making could improve.

5. Pause Before Acting

When facing a decision, take a moment to check in with yourself. Are you reacting emotionally, or thinking clearly?

A Real-Life Example

A CEO realized her preference for fast decisions often led to avoidable mistakes. By pausing to reflect and consulting her team, she became more deliberate and made better choices for the company's long-term goals.

Exercise

Think about a recent decision. Were any emotions or assumptions influencing your choice? Write down one way you could approach a similar situation with more self-awareness.

Takeaway

Self-awareness strengthens decision-making. Recognize your emotions, biases, and assumptions to approach problems with clarity and objectivity.

Chapter 57: Build Resilience

Setbacks are inevitable in problem-solving. Resilience is your ability to recover, adapt, and keep moving forward when things don't go as planned. It's not about avoiding failure—it's about learning from it and using it to grow stronger.

Resilience turns obstacles into opportunities, making you better equipped to handle future challenges.

How to Build Resilience

1. **Adopt a Growth Mindset**

   Treat failures as lessons. Ask, "What can I learn from this setback?"

2. **Stay Flexible**

   Be willing to adjust your plans when circumstances change. Rigidity leads to frustration; adaptability leads to progress.

3. **Focus on Your Strengths**

   Remind yourself of past challenges you've overcome. This builds confidence in your ability to handle new ones.

4. Find Support

Lean on friends, colleagues, or mentors for encouragement and advice during tough times.

5. Celebrate Small Wins

Acknowledge progress, no matter how small. Each step forward reinforces your resilience.

A Real-Life Example

A small business owner faced financial difficulties after losing a major client. Instead of giving up, she restructured her services, found new markets, and ultimately grew her business stronger than before.

Exercise

Write down one recent setback and what you learned from it. Then, identify one step you can take today to move forward with confidence.

Takeaway

Resilience turns failure into fuel. Learn, adapt, and keep moving forward to overcome challenges and grow stronger.

Chapter 58: Use Optimism Strategically

Optimism isn't just about seeing the bright side—it's about using hope and confidence to drive action. Strategic optimism means staying positive while remaining realistic about challenges. It's the balance between believing in a good outcome and preparing for obstacles along the way.

Optimism fuels motivation, encourages persistence, and helps you inspire others to tackle problems together.

How to Use Optimism Strategically

1. **Focus on Possibilities**

   Instead of dwelling on what could go wrong, focus on what could go right and how to achieve it.

2. **Acknowledge Challenges**

   Optimism doesn't mean ignoring risks. Identify obstacles and plan ways to address them.

3. Visualize Success

Picture the best-case scenario and use it as motivation to take action.

4. Spread Positivity

Optimism is contagious. Share your confidence with others to build a motivated, solution-focused team.

5. Stay Grounded in Reality

Balance your optimism with realistic planning. Hope drives action, but preparation ensures success.

A Real-Life Example

A non-profit leader used strategic optimism to rally her team during a funding crisis. By focusing on their mission and planning creatively, they found new donors and expanded their programs.

Exercise

Think of a challenge you're facing. Write down one reason to feel optimistic about the outcome and one action you can take to make it happen.

Takeaway

Optimism fuels action and inspires progress. Stay hopeful while planning realistically to overcome challenges with confidence.

Chapter 59: Respect Other Viewpoints

Respecting other viewpoints isn't just polite—it's essential for solving problems collaboratively. When you approach disagreements with an open mind, you uncover insights you might have missed and build stronger relationships.

Instead of focusing on who's "right," focus on understanding and integrating perspectives to find the best solution.

How to Respect Other Viewpoints

1. **Listen Actively**

   Pay attention to what others are saying, without interrupting or preparing your response.

2. **Ask Questions**

   Show curiosity by asking, "Why do you think that?" or "What's your perspective on this issue?"

3. Acknowledge Their Valid Points

Even if you disagree, recognize where the other person is coming from. For example, "I see why that's important to you."

4. Avoid Making It Personal

Focus on the issue, not the individual. Disagreeing with someone's idea doesn't mean rejecting them.

5. Find Common Ground

Identify areas where your perspectives overlap and use them as a foundation for collaboration.

A Real-Life Example

A marketing team debating an ad campaign found common ground by combining creative and data-driven approaches. Respecting each other's priorities led to a successful, balanced campaign.

Exercise

Think of a recent disagreement. Reflect on the other person's viewpoint and write down one valid point they made. Use this perspective to find a balanced solution.

Takeaway

Respecting other viewpoints strengthens collaboration. Listen, ask questions, and find common ground to create better solutions together.

Chapter 60: Stay Open to Feedback

Feedback isn't criticism — it's an opportunity to grow. Staying open to feedback means seeing it as a tool to improve your ideas, skills, and solutions. Even when feedback feels uncomfortable, it often reveals blind spots or new perspectives that make you better.

The key is to listen without defensiveness and use feedback constructively.

How to Stay Open to Feedback

1. **Invite Feedback Regularly**

   Proactively ask others for their thoughts on your work or approach.

2. **Listen Without Defensiveness**

   Focus on understanding the feedback instead of preparing a rebuttal.

3. **Ask for Specifics**

   General feedback like "This isn't working" isn't helpful. Ask for details to clarify what needs improvement.

4. **Thank the Feedback-Giver**

   Show appreciation for their input, even if you don't fully agree.

5. **Take Action**

   Use the feedback to refine your solution or process. Show others that their input made a difference.

A Real-Life Example

An app developer used early user feedback to identify confusing features in their design. By addressing these concerns, they improved usability and boosted customer satisfaction.

Exercise

Ask someone you trust for feedback on a current project or decision. Reflect on their input and write down one way you can use it to improve.

Takeaway

Feedback is a gift. Stay open, listen carefully, and use it to refine your approach for better results.

Section 7: Tools and Techniques

Every great problem-solver needs a toolkit. This section introduces practical methods to break down complex challenges, organize your thoughts, and find effective solutions. From visual tools like mind mapping and fishbone diagrams to structured techniques like SWOT analysis and prototyping, you'll learn how to apply proven strategies that make solving any problem easier and more efficient.

Chapter 61: SWOT Analysis Made Simple

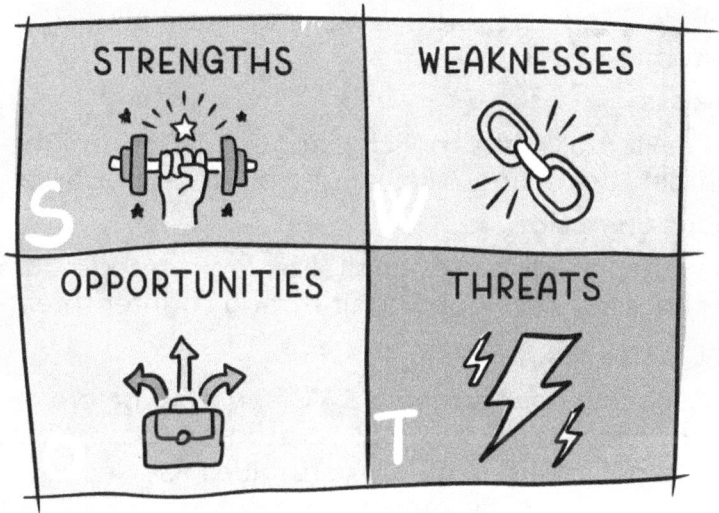

SWOT analysis is a simple yet powerful tool for evaluating any situation. By categorizing internal factors (strengths and weaknesses) and external factors (opportunities and threats), you get a clear, balanced view of where you stand and where to focus.

This method is especially useful for strategic planning, decision-making, and tackling challenges with multiple variables.

How to Use SWOT Analysis

1. **Strengths**

   Identify internal advantages. Ask, "What do we do well?" or "What resources give us an edge?" Examples might include strong leadership, unique skills, or loyal customers.

2. Weaknesses

Pinpoint internal areas that need improvement. Be honest about gaps in skills, resources, or processes that could hold you back.

3. Opportunities

Look for external factors that could benefit you. These could include market trends, emerging technologies, or unmet customer needs.

4. Threats

List external risks or challenges. These might include competitors, economic changes, or industry regulations.

5. Focus on Action

Use the insights to capitalize on strengths, minimize weaknesses, seize opportunities, and counter threats.

A Real-Life Example

A local bakery performed a SWOT analysis before expanding. Strengths included a loyal customer base; weaknesses highlighted limited staff. Opportunities lay in an untapped catering market, while a rising competitor was a clear threat. Their analysis led to hiring more staff and targeting catering, which boosted revenue.

Exercise

Choose a current project or challenge. Create a 2x2 grid and list at least two points for each SWOT category. Reflect on how this perspective shapes your strategy.

Takeaway

SWOT analysis clarifies your position by balancing strengths, weaknesses, opportunities, and threats. Use it to turn insights into actionable strategies.

Chapter 62: The Fishbone Diagram (Ishikawa)

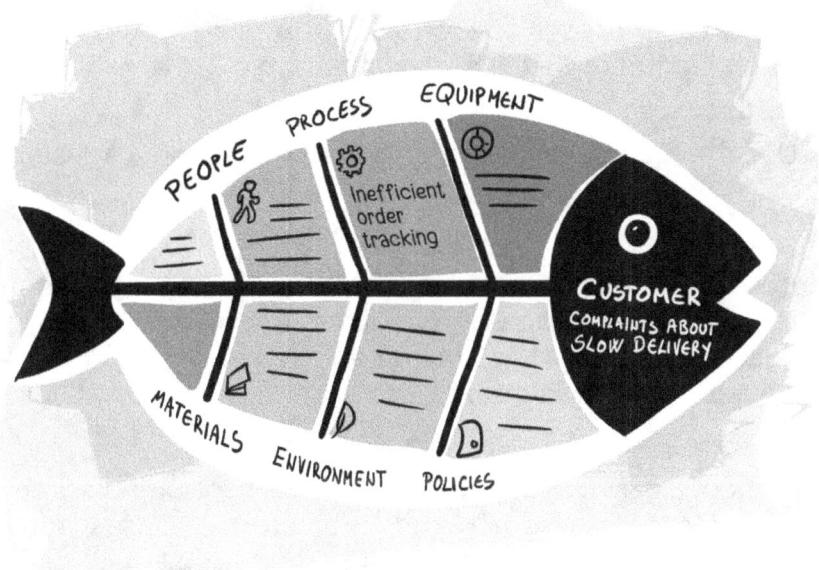

When a problem has multiple contributing factors, it's easy to get overwhelmed. The fishbone diagram, also known as the Ishikawa diagram, helps you organize potential causes visually, making it easier to identify the root issues. It's perfect for troubleshooting, process improvement, and quality control.

How to Use the Fishbone Diagram

1. **Define the Problem**

   Write the main issue at the "head" of the fish. For example, "Customer complaints about slow delivery."

2. **Identify Major Categories**

   Choose categories that might contribute to the problem. Common ones include People, Process, Equipment, Materials, Environment, and Policies.

3. **Brainstorm Causes**

    For each category, list possible contributing factors. For example, under "Process," you might include "inefficient order tracking."

4. **Analyze the Diagram**

    Review the causes to identify patterns or root issues. Focus on the factors most likely to drive improvement.

5. **Take Action**

    Use the insights to target and resolve the root causes.

A Real-Life Example

A manufacturing company used a fishbone diagram to address a rise in product defects. They found that most issues stemmed from outdated machinery under the "Equipment" category. Replacing the machines resolved the problem and improved production quality.

Exercise

Think of a recurring problem. Create a fishbone diagram with at least four categories and brainstorm causes for each. Highlight one or two root causes to address first.

Takeaway

The fishbone diagram helps you organize complex problems and pinpoint root causes. Break it down visually to uncover actionable solutions.

Chapter 63: Use the Five Whys

The Five Whys technique is a simple yet effective way to uncover the root cause of a problem. By asking "Why?" repeatedly (typically five times), you peel back the layers of symptoms to reveal the underlying issue. This method is quick, straightforward, and works for both personal and organizational challenges.

How to Use the Five Whys

1. **State the Problem Clearly**

   Start with a specific issue. For example, "Our sales are declining."

2. **Ask "Why?" Repeatedly**

   Each answer should lead to the next "Why." For example:
   - Why are sales declining? Customers are leaving.
   - Why are customers leaving? They're unhappy with support.
   - Why are they unhappy with support? Response times are too slow.

3. Stop at the Root Cause

Once you reach the fundamental issue, stop asking "Why?" and focus on fixing it.

4. Verify the Cause

Check whether addressing the root cause would prevent the problem from recurring.

5. Take Corrective Action

Implement a solution that targets the root cause, not just the symptoms.

A Real-Life Example

An IT department used the Five Whys to solve frequent system outages:

- Why are systems crashing? Servers are overloaded.
- Why are servers overloaded? Too many processes are running simultaneously.
- Why? There's no process to monitor usage.

They implemented a monitoring system, reducing outages by 80%.

Exercise

Choose a current challenge and apply the Five Whys. Write down each step and identify the root cause. Plan one action to address it.

Takeaway

The Five Whys dig beneath the surface to uncover root causes. Use it to avoid patching symptoms and solve problems at their core.

Chapter 64: Apply Design Thinking

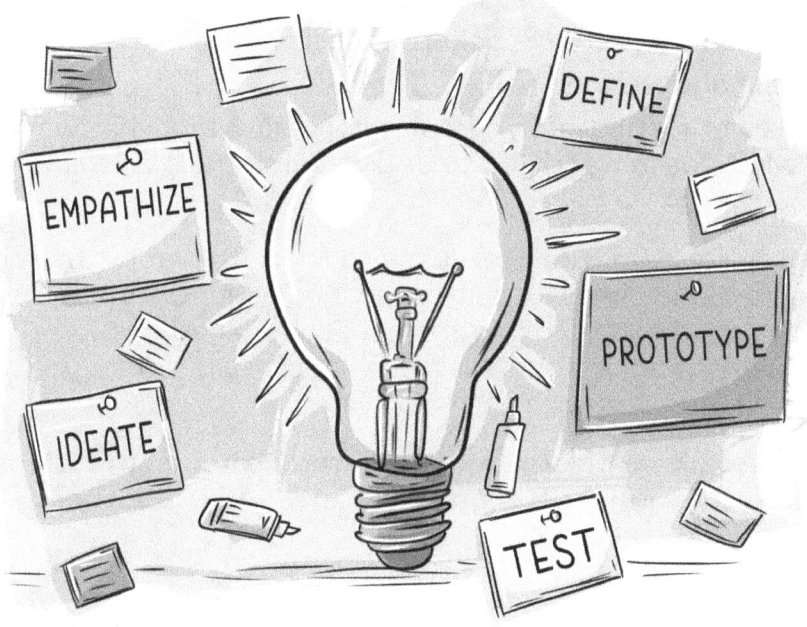

Design thinking is a human-centered approach to problem-solving that focuses on understanding user needs, generating creative ideas, and iterating solutions through testing. It's ideal for tackling ambiguous or complex challenges because it emphasizes empathy and experimentation.

How to Apply Design Thinking

1. **Empathize**

   Put yourself in the user's shoes. Conduct interviews, observe behaviors, or gather feedback to understand their needs and pain points.

2. **Define the Problem**

   Turn insights into a clear problem statement. For example: "How can we make onboarding simpler for new users?"

3. Ideate

Brainstorm as many ideas as possible without judgment. Encourage creativity and out-of-the-box thinking.

4. Prototype

Create a simple version of your idea to test quickly. This could be a sketch, mockup, or basic model.

5. Test and Refine

Gather feedback on the prototype, identify what works and what doesn't, and iterate until you find the best solution.

A Real-Life Example

A healthcare provider used design thinking to improve patient wait times. After observing patients and gathering feedback, they prototyped a new scheduling system. Testing revealed improvements that cut wait times by 50%.

Exercise

Choose a problem and walk through the five stages of design thinking. Focus on the user's needs and iterate until your solution feels right.

Takeaway

Design thinking puts users at the center of problem-solving. Empathize, brainstorm, and iterate to create solutions that truly work.

Chapter 65: Use Mind Mapping for Clarity

When problems feel chaotic or overwhelming, a mind map can bring order and clarity. Mind mapping is a visual technique for organizing ideas by branching them out from a central concept. It's especially helpful for brainstorming, simplifying complex problems, or exploring solutions in a structured yet creative way.

How to Use Mind Mapping for Problem-Solving

1. **Start with a Central Idea**

   Write the main problem or topic in the center of the page and draw a circle around it. For example, "Improve customer satisfaction."

2. **Branch Out Key Categories**

   Draw branches from the central circle for related categories. For example: "Customer Support," "Product Features," and "User Experience."

3. Add Subcategories and Ideas

Under each branch, jot down specific issues or solutions. For example, under "Customer Support," you might add "Response Times" and "Training."

4. Use Visual Elements

Add colors, icons, or drawings to highlight relationships or important points.

5. Review and Prioritize

Look at the completed mind map to identify patterns, prioritize key areas, or spot gaps in your thinking.

A Real-Life Example

A marketing team used mind mapping to plan a product launch. Starting with "Launch Strategy" at the center, they branched out into "Social Media," "Events," and "Ads." Each category included tasks, timelines, and key messages. The visual map helped them organize and execute the plan seamlessly.

Exercise

Take a problem you're currently working on. Create a mind map with at least three main branches and several subcategories. Review it to identify patterns or prioritize actions.

Takeaway

Mind mapping simplifies complexity by organizing ideas visually. Use it to see the big picture and uncover new connections in your problem-solving.

Chapter 66: Decision Matrix for Tough Choices

	Cost	Features	Long-Term Value	Score
Option A	4	2	3	9
Option B	3	4	5	12
Option C	2	4	2	8

When faced with multiple options, a decision matrix helps you compare them systematically. By scoring each option against key criteria, you eliminate bias and focus on the best overall choice. It's an ideal tool for complex decisions where many factors are at play.

How to Use a Decision Matrix

1. **List Your Options**

   Write down all the choices you're considering. For example, different job offers or software tools.

2. **Define Your Criteria**

   Identify the factors that matter most. For example: "Cost," "Ease of Use," and "Long-Term Value."

3. **Assign Weights to Criteria**

   Give each criterion a weight based on its importance. For example, "Cost" might be worth 40%, while "Ease of Use" is 30%.

4. Score Each Option

Rate each option against each criterion on a scale (e.g., 1 to 10). Multiply the scores by their respective weights.

5. Compare Total Scores

Add up the weighted scores for each option and choose the one with the highest total.

A Real-Life Example

A company choosing a new software platform used a decision matrix. They compared options based on "Cost," "Features," and "Scalability." After scoring each, the highest-scoring platform was selected, ensuring their choice aligned with long-term needs.

Exercise

Think of a decision you're facing. Create a decision matrix with at least three options and three criteria. Score and weigh each option to determine the best choice.

Takeaway

The decision matrix removes guesswork by evaluating choices objectively. Use it to tackle tough decisions with confidence and clarity.

Chapter 67: The Power of Prototyping

Prototyping is about testing your ideas early and often. Instead of waiting to perfect a solution, you build a simple version—whether it's a sketch, model, or mockup—and gather feedback. This iterative process lets you refine ideas quickly, saving time and resources in the long run.

How to Use Prototyping in Problem-Solving

1. **Start Simple**

   Create a basic, low-cost version of your idea. For example, use paper sketches, digital mockups, or rough models.

2. **Focus on Functionality**

   Your prototype doesn't have to be perfect. The goal is to test the core idea and identify what works or doesn't.

3. **Test with Real Users**

   Share your prototype with the people it's designed for. Gather feedback on their experience and suggestions for improvement.

4. Iterate and Improve

Use the feedback to refine your prototype. Each version brings you closer to the best solution.

5. Scale Up Gradually

Once the prototype works well, develop a more polished and complete version.

A Real-Life Example

A mobile app developer created wireframe prototypes to test new features with users. By identifying issues early, they avoided costly redesigns and launched an app with high user satisfaction.

Exercise

Think of a project or idea you're working on. Create a quick prototype (e.g. a sketch, mock-up, or small-scale version) and gather feedback from at least one person. Refine based on their input.

Takeaway

Prototyping helps you test ideas quickly and refine them with real feedback. Start small, iterate often, and build better solutions.

Chapter 68: Experimentation for Answers

Experimentation is one of the most effective ways to validate ideas and solve problems. By testing different approaches, observing results, and refining your methods, you learn what works best. Experiments are especially useful when data is unclear, or when innovation is required.

How to Experiment Effectively

1. **Define Your Hypothesis**

   Start with a clear question or assumption, like, "Will shorter emails improve response rates?"

2. **Design a Testable Experiment**

   Create a small, controlled test to gather insights. For example, send two versions of an email to different groups.

3. **Measure Results**

   Use metrics to evaluate outcomes. For instance, track open rates, click-throughs, or sales.

4. Analyze and Learn

Review the results to see if your hypothesis was correct. If not, adjust and try again.

5. Scale Successful Solutions

Once you've validated an approach, roll it out on a larger scale.

A Real-Life Example

A retailer experimented with different pricing strategies by offering discounts to a subset of customers. The experiment revealed that bundling discounts boosted sales more than individual markdowns, leading to a new pricing model.

Exercise

Identify a problem or idea and design a small experiment to test it. Write down your hypothesis, method, and what metrics you'll track. Conduct the test and analyze your results.

Takeaway

Experimentation uncovers what works through testing and observation. Try, learn, and refine to find the best solutions.

Chapter 69: Heuristics for Speed

Heuristics are mental shortcuts or rules of thumb that help you make decisions quickly without overthinking. They're especially useful when time is limited, or you're dealing with complex problems that don't require perfect accuracy. While heuristics don't always guarantee the best solution, they can guide you toward good enough answers efficiently.

By using heuristics wisely, you can save time, reduce analysis paralysis, and focus your energy where it matters most.

How to Use Heuristics for Problem-Solving

1. **Simplify Complex Decisions**

   Break down a decision into key factors and use a simple rule. For example: "If it's 80% good enough, move forward."

2. **Leverage Past Experience**

   Apply lessons from similar situations. For instance, if a past project succeeded by focusing on user feedback early, use that approach again.

3. **Use the Pareto Principle**

   Focus on the 20% of actions that will produce 80% of the results. This shortcut narrows your focus to what really matters.

4. **Prioritize with "Satisficing"**

   Instead of searching endlessly for the perfect solution, choose the first option that meets your key criteria.

5. **Be Mindful of Bias**

   While heuristics save time, they can sometimes introduce errors. Double-check critical decisions for blind spots.

A Real-Life Example

A hiring manager used the "rule of three" heuristic, interviewing three candidates before deciding whether to hire one or move on. This approach balanced efficiency with thoughtful evaluation, cutting hiring time in half without sacrificing quality.

Exercise

Think of a current decision that feels overwhelming. Write down a heuristic you could apply, like focusing on the most critical factor or setting a time limit for making the choice.

Takeaway

Heuristics simplify decision-making with practical shortcuts. Use them to act quickly while staying focused on what matters most.

Chapter 70: Algorithms and Flowcharts

When solving repetitive or process-heavy problems, algorithms and flowcharts bring clarity and structure. An algorithm is a step-by-step process for solving a problem, while a flowchart visually maps those steps. These tools help you streamline decisions, eliminate guesswork, and improve efficiency.

Algorithms and flowcharts are particularly helpful for tasks like troubleshooting, planning workflows, or training others.

How to Use Algorithms and Flowcharts

1. **Define the Goal**

   Start with a clear objective. For example, "Troubleshoot a slow internet connection."

2. **Break the Process Into Steps**

   Write down each action in order. For example:

   o Check if the router is plugged in.

   o Restart the router.

   o Call your internet provider.

3. Identify Decision Points

Highlight where choices must be made, like "Is the router light blinking?" or "Did restarting work?"

4. Draw the Flowchart

Use shapes and arrows to map the process visually. Show paths for different decisions or outcomes.

5. Test and Refine

Run through the algorithm or flowchart to ensure it works as intended. Adjust steps if needed.

A Real-Life Example

An IT help desk created a flowchart for resolving common technical issues. When employees called for support, the team followed the chart to troubleshoot efficiently. This reduced response times and improved satisfaction.

Exercise

Choose a recurring problem or process. Write down the steps needed to solve it and map them into a simple flowchart. Test it with a colleague or friend.

Takeaway

Algorithms and flowcharts streamline problem-solving by organizing steps into clear, repeatable processes. Use them to improve efficiency and reduce errors.

Section 8: Overcoming Cognitive Biases

Even the sharpest minds fall prey to cognitive biases—mental shortcuts and distortions that cloud judgment. These biases can lead to poor decisions, missed opportunities, or flawed problem-solving.

In this section, you'll learn how to recognize and overcome common biases like confirmation bias, the sunk cost fallacy, and overconfidence. By mastering these techniques, you'll improve your ability to think clearly, make balanced decisions, and solve problems effectively.

Chapter 71: Recognize Confirmation Bias

Confirmation bias happens when you only notice information that supports your beliefs while ignoring evidence that challenges them. It's comforting to find proof that we're "right," but this bias limits objectivity and leads to flawed decisions.

Recognizing confirmation bias allows you to step back, evaluate all evidence, and make decisions based on a full picture—not just the parts you agree with.

How to Avoid Confirmation Bias

1. **Actively Seek Contradictory Evidence**

   Challenge your viewpoint by asking, "What evidence would prove me wrong?" Look for it intentionally.

2. **Consider Alternative Perspectives**

   Ask someone with a different opinion to share their reasoning. Diverse viewpoints uncover blind spots.

3. Question Your Sources

Evaluate where your information comes from. Is it balanced or biased toward your preexisting beliefs?

4. Be Willing to Change Your Mind

Accepting new evidence isn't a weakness—it's a strength that leads to better decisions.

5. Use Data-Driven Analysis

Rely on objective data rather than personal opinions or anecdotal evidence.

A Real-Life Example

A hiring manager believed that candidates from prestigious universities performed better. However, by reviewing performance data, they found no significant difference between top schools and others. Recognizing their confirmation bias led to more equitable hiring practices.

Exercise

Think about a belief or decision you've made recently. Write down evidence that supports it, then actively search for evidence that challenges it. Reflect on whether this changes your perspective.

Takeaway

Confirmation bias narrows your vision. Challenge your assumptions and seek opposing evidence to make well-rounded decisions.

Chapter 72: Avoid the Sunk Cost Fallacy

The sunk cost fallacy traps you into sticking with decisions based on past investments of time, money, or effort—even when it no longer makes sense. It's hard to let go of what you've already poured into something, but clinging to a losing course only compounds the loss.

By recognizing sunk costs, you can make decisions based on future value, not past effort.

How to Avoid the Sunk Cost Fallacy

1. **Focus on the Present and Future**

   Ask, "If I hadn't invested in this already, would I still make the same choice today?"

2. **Separate Emotion from Logic**

   Acknowledge any emotional attachment to your past investment, then set it aside to think clearly.

3. Reevaluate Regularly

Periodically reassess whether your current path is still the best option.

4. Learn to Walk Away

Accept that letting go isn't failure—it's making room for better opportunities.

5. Reframe Losses as Lessons

Treat sunk costs as valuable learning experiences rather than wasted resources.

A Real-Life Example

A start-up invested heavily in a product that wasn't gaining traction. Despite mounting losses, they hesitated to pivot. When they finally shifted focus to a more promising idea, they found success. Recognizing the sunk cost fallacy helped them move forward.

Exercise

Think of a project or decision where you feel stuck. Ask yourself, "Am I continuing this only because of past investment?" Write down one action to focus on future gains instead.

Takeaway

Let go of sunk costs and focus on what adds value going forward. Decisions should prioritize future opportunities, not past investments.

Chapter 73: Fight Availability Heuristics

The availability heuristic leads you to base decisions on information that's easiest to recall—like vivid memories, recent events, or dramatic stories—rather than factual data. While quick, this shortcut often distorts reality and prevents sound judgment.

By recognizing this bias, you can rely on more objective evidence instead of relying on what's simply memorable.

How to Fight Availability Heuristics

1. **Seek Out Data**

   Before making decisions, look for statistics, reports, or research that provide a more balanced view.

2. **Question Emotional Responses**

   Ask, "Am I focusing on this because it's relevant or just because it's memorable?"

3. Broaden Your Perspective

Consider multiple examples or case studies, not just the most striking ones.

4. Use a Checklist

Structured decision-making tools can help ensure all factors are considered, not just the most memorable ones.

5. Review the Bigger Picture

Step back and assess whether your decision reflects broader trends or isolated incidents.

A Real-Life Example

A CEO almost scrapped a product after one high-profile customer complained. However, data showed that most customers were satisfied. Ignoring the availability heuristic helped the company avoid an overreaction and keep a successful product in the market.

Exercise

Think of a recent decision where you relied on a vivid example. Find objective data to check whether your judgment was accurate. Reflect on how this changes your view.

Takeaway

The most memorable information isn't always the most reliable. Rely on data and broader trends to avoid the traps of availability heuristics.

Chapter 74: Control Anchoring Effects

Anchoring bias happens when your decisions are overly influenced by the first piece of information you encounter. Whether it's an initial price, a single opinion, or a past estimate, this "anchor" can skew your thinking and block better choices.

By controlling anchoring effects, you can evaluate options more fairly and make better-informed decisions.

How to Control Anchoring Effects

1. **Delay Judgment**

   Avoid making decisions until you've reviewed all relevant information.

2. **Consider Multiple Anchors**

   Compare several starting points rather than fixating on just one.

3. Challenge the Initial Anchor

Ask yourself, "Why am I basing my decision on this number or idea? Does it truly reflect reality?"

4. Use Independent Estimates

Get input from unbiased sources to counteract the influence of the initial anchor.

5. Revisit the Problem

Step back from the anchor and reassess your decision with a fresh perspective.

A Real-Life Example

A car buyer negotiating a price was anchored by the dealer's high initial offer. After researching fair market values and setting their own target price, they negotiated a much better deal.

Exercise

Think of a decision where an initial number or idea influenced you. Reassess it by gathering additional information or creating a new starting point.

Takeaway

Anchors can bias your decisions. Challenge initial information and seek alternative starting points to make more balanced choices.

Chapter 75: Beware of Overconfidence Bias

Overconfidence bias occurs when you overestimate your skills, knowledge, or ability to predict outcomes. While confidence is important, too much of it can lead to risky decisions, ignoring potential pitfalls, or underpreparing for challenges.

Recognizing overconfidence allows you to stay humble, ask for input, and make more informed choices.

How to Avoid Overconfidence Bias

1. **Check Your Assumptions**

   Ask, "What facts support my belief?" and "What might I be overlooking?"

2. **Seek Feedback**

   Consult others for their perspective. External opinions often reveal blind spots.

3. **Consider Worst-Case Scenarios**

   Evaluate what could go wrong and how you'd handle it.

4. **Test Your Ideas**

   Instead of assuming success, run small experiments to validate your approach before fully committing.

5. **Embrace Lifelong Learning**

   Acknowledge that there's always more to learn, even in areas where you excel.

A Real-Life Example

A seasoned investor was so confident in a single stock pick that he ignored market warnings. When the stock tanked, he lost heavily. Learning from this, he adopted a diversified strategy and sought input from other experts, improving his future performance.

Exercise

Think of a decision where you felt overconfident. Write down potential risks or gaps in your knowledge and one way to address them.

Takeaway

Confidence is valuable, but overconfidence blinds you to risks. Stay humble, seek input, and prepare for challenges to make smarter decisions.

Chapter 76: Manage Decision Fatigue

Decision fatigue happens when you're overwhelmed by too many choices, leading to poor decisions, procrastination, or burnout. Your mental energy is a finite resource, and each decision you make depletes it.

Managing decision fatigue helps you preserve your focus for what truly matters.

How to Manage Decision Fatigue

1. **Prioritize Important Decisions**

   Tackle high-stakes decisions early in the day when your mind is freshest.

2. **Simplify Routine Choices**

   Automate or streamline low-priority decisions, like meal planning or daily tasks.

3. Limit Options

Reduce the number of choices you consider. For example, shortlist three options instead of ten.

4. Take Breaks

Rest and recharge your mental energy before tackling more decisions.

5. Plan Ahead

Make decisions in advance when possible, such as creating a weekly schedule or setting goals.

A Real-Life Example

A CEO simplified her daily routine by delegating minor tasks and setting a standard work wardrobe. By reducing small decisions, she saved energy for strategic planning and problem-solving.

Exercise

Identify one area of your life where decision fatigue is affecting you. Streamline or automate one type of routine decision to reduce mental overload.

Takeaway

Decision fatigue drains mental energy. Simplify, prioritize, and automate to stay focused on what matters most.

Chapter 77: Combat Group Polarization

Group polarization occurs when teams take increasingly extreme positions after group discussions. Instead of finding balance, members reinforce each other's views, leading to risky decisions or unnecessary conflict.

Preventing group polarization ensures more measured, rational, and collaborative outcomes.

How to Combat Group Polarization

1. **Encourage Diverse Perspectives**

    Actively invite input from members with different viewpoints to counterbalance extremes.

2. **Play Devil's Advocate**

    Assign someone to challenge the group's assumptions and encourage critical thinking.

3. Break Into Smaller Groups

Smaller groups tend to stay more balanced and focused than large, unanimous ones.

4. Focus on Evidence

Ground discussions in facts and data rather than opinions or emotions.

5. Review the Decision Independently

Ask each member to reflect privately on the group's decision before finalizing it.

A Real-Life Example

A company brainstorming marketing strategies veered toward an extreme "all-in" risky campaign. A team member playing devil's advocate highlighted the risks, leading to a balanced strategy that incorporated boldness with safeguards.

Exercise

Think of a group decision you were part of. Reflect on whether the group leaned too far toward one extreme and how you could encourage balance in future discussions.

Takeaway

Group polarization skews decisions. Encourage balance by seeking diverse views, grounding discussions in evidence, and challenging extreme positions.

Chapter 78: Recognize the Dunning-Kruger Effect

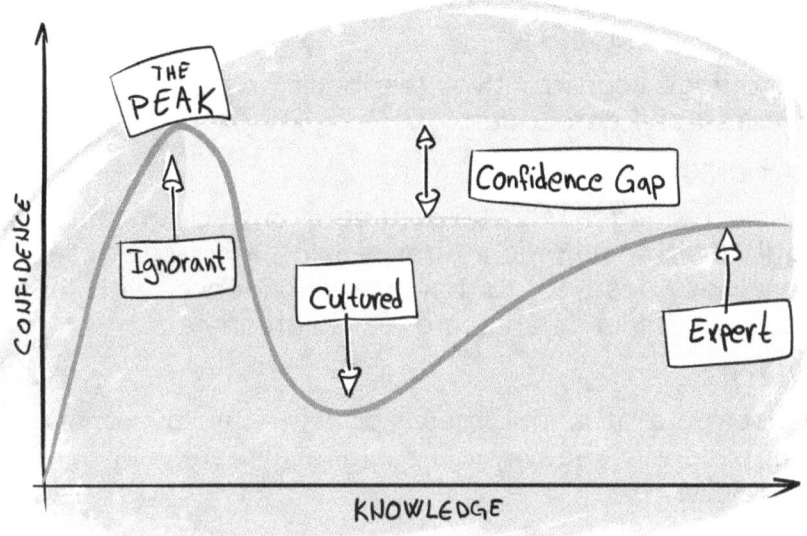

The Dunning-Kruger Effect describes how people with little knowledge overestimate their competence, while experts often underestimate theirs. This bias can lead to misplaced confidence or hesitation to act when you're actually capable. Recognizing this effect helps you accurately assess your abilities and seek help when needed.

How to Recognize and Manage the Dunning-Kruger Effect

1. **Be Honest About Your Knowledge**

   Reflect on whether your confidence matches your actual expertise.

2. **Seek Feedback from Experts**

   Ask someone more experienced for their perspective to calibrate your self-assessment.

3. Keep Learning

The more you learn, the more aware you become of what you don't know.

4. Balance Confidence with Humility

Trust your skills while staying open to new insights and growth.

5. Help Others Avoid It

Encourage constructive feedback in teams to ensure accurate self-perception.

A Real-Life Example

A new manager felt overconfident in decision-making but struggled with delegation. After seeking advice from seasoned leaders, they learned to balance confidence with humility, improving both leadership and team outcomes.

Exercise

Reflect on a situation where you felt either overconfident or hesitant. Identify one way you could recalibrate your perception of your skills.

Takeaway

The Dunning-Kruger Effect distorts self-perception. Stay humble, seek feedback, and embrace learning to align confidence with competence.

Chapter 79: Counteract Framing Effects

Framing effects occur when decisions are influenced by how information is presented rather than the facts themselves. For example, describing a product as "90% effective" sounds more appealing than "10% failure rate," even though they mean the same thing. Recognizing framing effects helps you focus on substance over presentation, leading to more objective decisions.

How to Counteract Framing Effects

1. **Reframe the Situation**

   Rewrite the problem or decision in different ways. Ask, "How would this look framed differently?"

2. **Focus on Facts, Not Phrasing**

   Strip away the language and evaluate the raw data or numbers.

3. Consider Both Sides

Look at both the positive and negative framing to balance your view.

4. Question the Messenger's Intent

Ask, "Why is this being presented this way? What's the goal behind the framing?"

5. Take a Step Back

Give yourself time to process the information without rushing to judgment.

A Real-Life Example

A health campaign presented a procedure as "90% successful," leading to high patient acceptance. When reframed as "10% failure," patients hesitated. Recognizing the framing helped balance communication and build trust.

Exercise

Think of a recent decision influenced by how information was framed. Reframe the same information differently and evaluate how it changes your perspective.

Takeaway

Framing can distort perception. Focus on the facts behind the presentation to make objective, informed decisions.

Chapter 80: Balance Intuition with Analysis

Intuition and analysis both play important roles in decision-making. Intuition, based on experience and subconscious patterns, can provide quick insights. Analysis, rooted in facts and data, ensures logic and objectivity. Balancing the two leads to better problem-solving by combining instinct with evidence.

How to Balance Intuition and Analysis

1. **Start with Your Gut**

   Reflect on your initial instinct about the problem. What feels right, and why?

2. **Follow Up with Data**

   Test your intuition against data or research to ensure it aligns with reality.

3. **Be Wary of Bias**

   Recognize when emotions or personal preferences might skew your intuition.

4. **Use Intuition for Speed, Analysis for Accuracy**

When time is short, rely on intuition. For critical decisions, prioritize analysis.

5. **Refine Intuition Through Experience**

The more you reflect on past decisions, the sharper your intuition becomes.

A Real-Life Example

A marketing director had a gut feeling that a new campaign idea would resonate. Instead of acting immediately, she tested the concept with focus groups. The data confirmed her instincts, leading to a successful launch.

Exercise

Think about a decision where you relied solely on intuition or analysis. Reflect on how using the other approach might have improved the outcome.

Takeaway

Intuition offers speed; analysis provides accuracy. Balance both to make decisions that are both insightful and evidence-based.

Section 9: Resilience in Problem-Solving

Resilience is the backbone of effective problem-solving. It's the ability to bounce back, adapt, and persist even in the face of setbacks or uncertainty. In this section, you'll learn how to transform failure into growth, pivot strategies when necessary, and stay focused on your goals while embracing patience and adaptability. Resilient problem-solvers don't just survive challenges—they thrive because of them.

Chapter 81: Learn from Failure

Failure is not the opposite of success—it's part of the journey toward it. Every mistake or setback carries lessons that can refine your approach and improve future outcomes. Learning from failure requires reflection, humility, and the willingness to adapt.

How to Learn from Failure

1. **Own Your Mistakes**

   Acknowledge what went wrong without defensiveness. Accountability is the first step toward growth.

2. **Analyze the Cause**

   Break down what led to the failure. Was it a lack of preparation, a flawed strategy, or external factors?

3. **Focus on Lessons, Not Blame**

   Shift your perspective from "What went wrong?" to "What can I do better next time?"

4. **Adjust Your Approach**

    Use what you've learned to improve your strategy or decision-making process.

5. **Move Forward**

    Don't dwell on the setback. Treat it as a stepping stone and keep pushing toward your goal.

A Real-Life Example

A tech startup launched a product that failed to gain traction. Instead of giving up, the team analyzed customer feedback and realized their marketing wasn't reaching the right audience. They refined their strategy and relaunched, eventually achieving success.

Exercise

Think of a recent failure. Write down three lessons you learned and one specific change you can make to avoid repeating the mistake.

Takeaway

Failure is a powerful teacher. Reflect, learn, and adapt to turn setbacks into stepping stones toward success.

Chapter 82: Pivot, Don't Quit

Sometimes, the path you're on isn't leading to success — but that doesn't mean you should abandon your goal. Pivoting means adjusting your strategy while keeping the end goal in sight. It's a powerful way to adapt to challenges without giving up entirely.

How to Pivot Effectively

1. **Recognize When It's Time to Change**

   If progress stalls or circumstances shift, evaluate whether your current approach is still viable.

2. **Reassess Your Goal**

   Ask, "Is the goal still worth pursuing?" If yes, focus on finding a new path to achieve it.

3. **Identify What's Working**

   Pinpoint the elements of your current strategy that are effective and keep them in your revised plan.

4. Explore New Approaches

Brainstorm alternative methods or strategies to move forward.

5. Commit to the New Direction

Once you've decided to pivot, fully embrace the new approach without hesitation.

A Real-Life Example

Instagram started as a location-based app called Burbn. When the founders realized users were primarily sharing photos, they pivoted to focus on photo-sharing, leading to the Instagram we know today.

Exercise

Think of a goal where you've hit a roadblock. Write down one aspect you can change or improve while keeping the bigger picture in mind.

Takeaway

Pivoting keeps you moving forward when the original plan falters. Adapt your strategy without losing sight of your goal.

Chapter 83: Stay Adaptive to Change

Change is inevitable, and rigid plans often break under its weight. Staying adaptive means being ready to shift gears, embrace new circumstances, and adjust your approach as needed. Flexibility allows you to thrive in uncertainty and turn unexpected challenges into opportunities.

How to Stay Adaptive

1. **Monitor Your Environment**

   Stay aware of trends, feedback, and changes that could impact your goals.

2. **Embrace a Growth Mindset**

   See change as an opportunity to learn and grow, rather than a threat to your plans.

3. **Stay Open to New Ideas**

   Be willing to try alternative methods, even if they deviate from your original plan.

4. Prepare for Multiple Scenarios

Anticipate different outcomes and have contingency plans ready.

5. Stay Calm in Uncertainty

Focus on what you can control and remain flexible in areas that you can't.

A Real-Life Example

A restaurant facing reduced dine-in traffic during the pandemic quickly adapted by expanding takeout and delivery options. Their ability to pivot kept the business afloat and even grew their customer base.

Exercise

Identify a situation where circumstances have changed recently. Write down one adjustment you can make to adapt and stay on track.

Takeaway

Adaptability is the key to thriving in a changing world. Stay flexible, embrace new opportunities, and adjust your approach as needed.

Chapter 84: Build a Feedback Loop

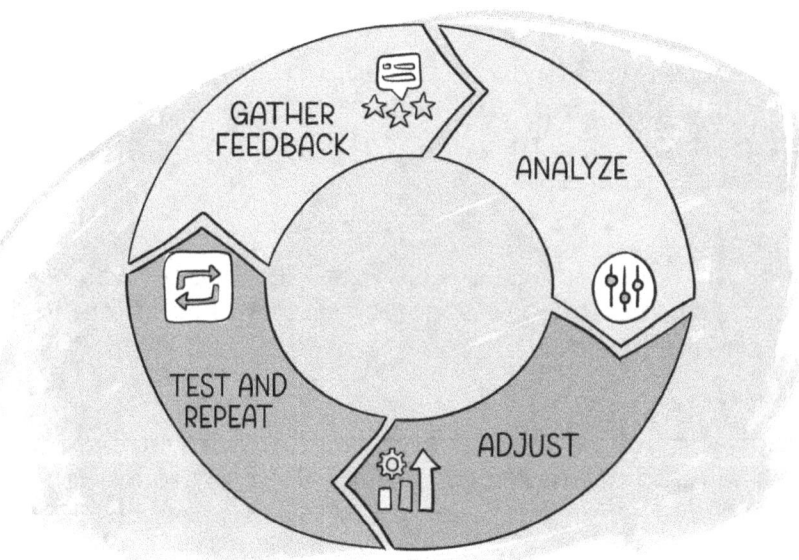

Feedback loops are essential for continuous improvement. By regularly collecting input, analyzing results, and making adjustments, you can refine your solutions and achieve better outcomes over time. A strong feedback loop turns one-time successes into lasting progress.

How to Build a Feedback Loop

1. **Gather Input Regularly**

   Collect feedback from users, team members, or stakeholders at every stage.

2. **Analyze the Data**

   Look for patterns or recurring issues in the feedback.

3. **Make Adjustments**

   Use the insights to refine your approach, whether it's improving processes, products, or strategies.

4. **Test the Changes**

   Implement adjustments and evaluate their effectiveness.

5. **Repeat the Process**

   Feedback isn't a one-time activity—it's an ongoing cycle of learning and improving.

A Real-Life Example

A software company built a feedback loop by releasing beta versions of their app and collecting user reviews. Iterating based on feedback, they launched a polished product that exceeded user expectations.

Exercise

Think of a project or goal. Write down one way you can gather feedback and one specific adjustment you could make based on what you learn.

Takeaway

Feedback loops drive continuous improvement. Collect input, make adjustments, and refine your approach for lasting success.

Chapter 85: Recognize When to Let Go

Not every problem can be solved, and not every goal is worth pursuing forever. Recognizing when to let go frees up your energy and resources for challenges with better potential outcomes. Letting go isn't failure—it's a strategic choice to focus on what truly matters.

How to Recognize When to Let Go

1. **Assess the Impact**

   Ask, "If I solved this problem, would the result still be worth the effort?"

2. **Evaluate Your Resources**

   Determine whether continuing is draining time, energy, or money that could be better spent elsewhere.

3. **Listen to Feedback**

   If others consistently point out that a problem may not be solvable, consider their perspective.

4. Reflect on Your Goals

Ask, "Is this still aligned with my bigger objectives?"

5. Shift Your Focus

Channel your energy into more achievable or impactful challenges.

A Real-Life Example

A business owner struggling to revive a failing product line decided to discontinue it and focus on their best-selling items instead. This decision freed up resources and led to record profits.

Exercise

Think of a problem you've been holding onto. Reflect on whether solving it is still worth the effort, and identify one area where you could redirect your focus instead.

Takeaway

Letting go isn't giving up—it's making space for better opportunities. Focus on problems and goals that truly matter.

Chapter 86: Embrace Experimentation

Experimentation is a cornerstone of resilient problem-solving. Instead of waiting for the perfect solution, testing ideas early and learning from the results allows you to refine your approach. By embracing experimentation, you create a culture of progress over perfection, turning uncertainty into discovery.

How to Embrace Experimentation

1. **Start Small**

   Test your idea on a small scale to minimize risks while gathering valuable insights.

2. **Define Success Metrics**

   Decide what outcomes will indicate success or failure before starting the experiment.

3. **Document Results**

   Track what worked, what didn't, and why. Detailed observations help you make better adjustments.

4. **Iterate and Improve**

   Use what you've learned to refine the next version of your solution.

5. **Accept Failure as Feedback**

   Treat failed experiments as opportunities to learn, not as setbacks.

A Real-Life Example

A clothing brand used A/B testing to experiment with different website layouts. By measuring click-through rates and sales, they discovered which design worked best, leading to a 25% increase in conversions.

Exercise

Think of an idea or solution you want to test. Design a small experiment, write down success metrics, and outline how you'll use the results to improve.

Takeaway

Experimentation fuels progress. Test early, learn constantly, and refine your approach to build better solutions.

Chapter 87: Cultivate Patience in Uncertainty

Uncertainty can feel overwhelming, especially when results aren't immediate. Patience is the ability to stay calm and focused while waiting for progress to unfold. Cultivating patience doesn't mean doing nothing—it means trusting the process and staying persistent even when outcomes aren't clear.

How to Cultivate Patience in Uncertainty

1. **Focus on What You Can Control**

   Instead of worrying about unknowns, channel your energy into actions that move you forward.

2. **Break Goals Into Milestones**

   Small, measurable achievements help you see progress, even during long-term projects.

3. Practice Mindfulness

Stay grounded in the present moment rather than fixating on future outcomes.

4. Remind Yourself of the Bigger Picture

Keep your long-term goals in mind to maintain motivation through slow progress.

5. Celebrate Progress

Acknowledge small wins to stay positive and resilient.

A Real-Life Example

An author working on a novel struggled with uncertainty about its reception. By focusing on daily word count goals and celebrating small milestones, they completed the book and ultimately found success.

Exercise

Think of a project where you're facing uncertainty. Write down one small milestone you can achieve this week to maintain momentum.

Takeaway

Patience turns uncertainty into opportunity. Stay focused on progress, trust the process, and persist through the unknown.

Chapter 88: Keep Your Eye on the Goal

In problem-solving, it's easy to get side-tracked by setbacks, distractions, or minor details. Keeping your eye on the goal means staying focused on what matters most, even when obstacles arise. By regularly reconnecting with your purpose, you ensure that every action aligns with your ultimate objective.

How to Stay Focused on the Goal

1. **Define Your Purpose Clearly**

   Write down your goal and why it's important to you or your team.

2. **Regularly Revisit Your Goal**

   Set reminders or check-ins to ensure your actions remain aligned with your objective.

3. **Ignore Distractions**

   Learn to distinguish between tasks that support your goal and those that pull you off track.

4. **Adapt Without Losing Sight**

   Be flexible in your methods, but always keep the end result in mind.

5. **Celebrate the Journey**

   Acknowledge the progress you've made so far to stay motivated.

A Real-Life Example

A non-profit aiming to raise funds for a new initiative faced unexpected hurdles. By focusing on their mission and adapting strategies, they surpassed their fundraising target while staying true to their purpose.

Exercise

Write down your current goal and one action you can take today to move closer to achieving it.

Takeaway

Focus on your destination. Stay adaptable, avoid distractions, and reconnect with your purpose to achieve your goals.

Chapter 89: Trust the Process

When faced with challenges, it's easy to doubt whether your efforts will pay off. Trusting the process means having confidence in your problem-solving framework and taking consistent action, even when results aren't immediate.

How to Trust the Process

1. **Have a Clear Plan**

   A well-thought-out strategy provides the structure to guide your efforts.

2. **Focus on Consistency**

   Small, steady actions often lead to big results over time.

3. **Stay Flexible**

   Adjust your approach as needed, but remain committed to the overall process.

4. **Measure Progress**

   Track milestones and use them as proof that your efforts are working.

5. Resist Impatience

Remind yourself that meaningful change takes time and persistence.

A Real-Life Example

A fitness enthusiast focused on consistent daily workouts and trusted their plan, even when early results were minimal. Over months, their dedication paid off with noticeable improvements in strength and endurance.

Exercise

Identify a process you're following. Write down one reason to trust it and one adjustment you can make to improve it.

Takeaway

Success is built on consistency. Trust your process, take steady action, and adjust as needed to achieve long-term results.

Chapter 90: Celebrate Small Wins

Big goals often feel daunting, but celebrating small wins along the way keeps you motivated and builds momentum. Each milestone represents progress and reinforces your ability to achieve the final goal. Recognizing these moments fuels your energy and strengthens resilience.

How to Celebrate Small Wins

1. **Set Mini-Milestones**

   Break your larger goal into smaller, achievable steps to track progress.

2. **Acknowledge Each Achievement**

   Take a moment to reflect on and appreciate your progress, no matter how small.

3. **Reward Yourself**

   Celebrate milestones with simple rewards, like a break, a treat, or sharing your success with others.

4. Share Wins with Your Team

If you're working collaboratively, highlight group achievements to boost morale.

5. Use Wins as Motivation

Let each success inspire you to keep moving forward.

A Real-Life Example

A student writing a thesis celebrated each completed chapter with a small reward, like a favorite snack. These celebrations kept them motivated to tackle the next section and finish their project.

Exercise

Think of a recent milestone you've reached. Write down one way you can celebrate it and one next step to build on your momentum.

Takeaway

Small wins lead to big victories. Celebrate milestones to stay motivated, build momentum, and enjoy the journey toward your goal.

Section 10: Advanced Problem-Solving

Problem-solving at the highest level requires advanced tools and mindsets. This section explores techniques to help you tackle complex and dynamic challenges. You'll learn to anticipate the future, embrace constraints, and balance logic with creativity. Whether you're refining your process or exploring innovative approaches, these strategies will elevate your problem-solving to mastery.

Chapter 91: Apply Game Theory

Game theory is the study of strategic decision-making, especially in situations where others' actions affect your outcomes. Whether you're negotiating, competing, or collaborating, game theory helps you predict and influence behaviors by considering everyone's interests and potential moves.

How to Use Game Theory in Problem-Solving

1. **Define the Players**

   Identify all the key players involved in the problem, including yourself, competitors, and collaborators.

2. **Understand Motivations**

   Determine what each player wants and what drives their decisions.

3. **Predict Actions**

   Consider how others are likely to act based on their goals and constraints.

4. Analyze Possible Outcomes

Map out scenarios for each combination of actions to anticipate the best and worst results.

5. Choose Strategic Moves

Make decisions that maximize your outcome while minimizing risks, often by influencing others' choices.

A Real-Life Example

During a price war, a company analyzed competitors' likely responses to various pricing strategies. By predicting that competitors wouldn't sustain long-term discounts, they chose a steady pricing strategy, retaining profits while competitors faltered.

Exercise

Think of a situation where other people's actions affect your outcomes. List their potential moves and plan one strategic decision based on likely scenarios.

Takeaway

Game theory sharpens your strategic thinking. Anticipate others' actions and plan your moves to achieve the best outcomes.

Chapter 92: Master First-Principles Thinking

First-principles thinking is a powerful method of solving problems by breaking them down into their most fundamental truths. Instead of relying on assumptions or existing methods, you rebuild solutions from the ground up, enabling innovative approaches and fresh perspectives.

How to Apply First-Principles Thinking

1. Identify Assumptions

List everything you believe about the problem. For example, "This product must be expensive to produce."

2. Question Each Assumption

Ask, "Is this really true? Why?" Challenge conventional wisdom to find overlooked possibilities.

3. Break It Down

Reduce the problem to its simplest components. For example, "What are the raw materials? What is their actual cost?"

4. Rebuild with New Insights

Use the fundamentals to create a more efficient, innovative solution.

5. Repeat as Needed

Apply this process regularly to uncover breakthroughs in thinking.

A Real-Life Example

Elon Musk used first-principles thinking to cut rocket costs at SpaceX. Instead of buying prebuilt components, the team analyzed raw materials and built rockets in-house for a fraction of the cost.

Exercise

Choose a problem and list your assumptions about it. Break the problem into basic elements and brainstorm one solution based on these fundamentals.

Takeaway

First-principles thinking challenges assumptions and rebuilds solutions from the ground up. Use it to unlock innovative answers.

Chapter 93: Leverage Bayesian Thinking

I'm sure this ad campaign will work—it worked last year.

But we have new data now. Let's update our assumptions.

Bayesian thinking helps you make better decisions by continuously updating your beliefs as new evidence emerges. It's not about being "right" or "wrong" initially—it's about refining your understanding over time through logic and probability.

How to Use Bayesian Thinking

1. **Start with a Prior Belief**

   Begin with an initial assumption or hypothesis based on current knowledge.

2. **Gather New Evidence**

   Seek data or information that supports or challenges your belief.

3. **Update Your Belief**

   Adjust your assumption based on the strength and relevance of the new evidence.

4. Repeat as Needed

Continuously refine your understanding as more evidence becomes available.

5. Apply Probability

Use likelihoods instead of certainties. For example, "This solution has a 70% chance of success based on the data."

A Real-Life Example

A doctor diagnosing a patient begins with a likely cause based on symptoms. As test results arrive, they adjust their diagnosis, increasing or decreasing the probability of each potential condition until the most accurate conclusion is reached.

Exercise

Think of a belief or decision you've made recently. Identify one piece of new evidence that could challenge or refine it, and update your thinking accordingly.

Takeaway

Bayesian thinking refines decisions by incorporating new evidence. Update your beliefs continuously for better outcomes.

Chapter 94: Use Scenario Analysis for Complexity

Complex problems often have uncertain outcomes, but scenario analysis prepares you for multiple possibilities. By imagining different futures and planning responses to each, you build resilience and adaptability into your decision-making process.

How to Use Scenario Analysis

1. **Define the Problem**

   Identify a challenge with uncertain outcomes. For example, "How will market conditions affect our product launch?"

2. **Identify Key Variables**

   List factors that could influence outcomes, like customer behavior, competition, or economic trends.

3. **Create Scenarios**

   Develop a few plausible scenarios, such as "Best Case," "Worst Case," and "Most Likely."

4. Plan Responses

Outline actions you'd take for each scenario to mitigate risks or seize opportunities.

5. Review and Adapt

Revisit your scenarios periodically as conditions evolve.

A Real-Life Example

A retail chain planning for economic uncertainty developed three scenarios: economic growth, stagnation, and recession. By preparing tailored strategies for each, they successfully adapted to a challenging market.

Exercise

Choose a current challenge and outline three possible scenarios. Write down one action you'd take for each to stay prepared.

Takeaway

Scenario analysis prepares you for uncertainty. Plan for multiple outcomes to stay adaptable and resilient.

Chapter 95: Explore Contrarian Solutions

Sometimes the best solutions lie in doing the opposite of what's expected. Contrarian thinking challenges conventional wisdom, encouraging you to explore ideas others might dismiss. By questioning norms, you unlock creative and unexpected solutions.

How to Explore Contrarian Solutions

1. **Question the Status Quo**

   Ask, "Why do we always do it this way?" and "What if we tried the opposite?"

2. **Seek Out Unpopular Opinions**

   Listen to ideas that go against the majority—they might reveal overlooked opportunities.

3. **Challenge Assumptions**

   Test whether commonly accepted beliefs hold up under scrutiny.

4. **Combine the Contrarian with the Practical**

   Blend bold ideas with actionable steps to make them realistic.

5. **Stay Open to Risk**

   Contrarian solutions often carry uncertainty, but they can lead to breakthroughs when executed well.

A Real-Life Example

Netflix's decision to focus on streaming, instead of expanding DVD rentals like competitors, was a contrarian move that disrupted the entertainment industry and defined the future of media.

Exercise

Think of a problem where the usual approach isn't working. Write down one contrarian solution and consider how you might test it.

Takeaway

Contrarian thinking challenges norms and unlocks innovation. Dare to explore unconventional solutions for bold breakthroughs.

Chapter 96: Think Like a Futurist

Thinking like a futurist means looking beyond the present to anticipate trends, innovations, and disruptions that could shape the future. By understanding the big picture, you can make strategic decisions today that prepare you for tomorrow's challenges and opportunities. Futurist thinking combines creativity, data, and foresight to build adaptable, forward-thinking strategies.

How to Think Like a Futurist

1. **Study Emerging Trends**

   Pay attention to advancements in technology, shifts in culture, and changes in global systems.

2. **Ask "What If?"**

   Imagine future scenarios, from optimistic to catastrophic, and consider their implications.

3. **Focus on Long-Term Goals**

   Look beyond immediate results and ask, "How will this decision play out five, ten, or twenty years from now?"

4. **Prepare for Disruption**

   Think about how current industries or practices could be radically changed by new developments.

5. **Collaborate Across Fields**

   Work with people from diverse industries to gain a broader perspective on potential futures.

A Real-Life Example

Amazon's investment in cloud computing through AWS in the early 2000s was a futurist move. They anticipated the growing need for scalable online storage and built an industry-leading platform, which became a major revenue source.

Exercise

Choose an area of interest or work. Research one emerging trend and write down how it could affect your field in the next decade. Identify one way to prepare for it.

Takeaway

Thinking like a futurist helps you anticipate change and stay ahead of the curve. Look beyond the present to shape a resilient, forward-looking strategy.

Chapter 97: Use Constraints to Your Advantage

Constraints—whether they're time, money, or resources—can feel like roadblocks, but they're often the spark for creative breakthroughs. By working within limitations, you're forced to think differently, prioritize, and innovate. Constraints don't just restrict—they focus your efforts and push you to find smarter, leaner solutions.

How to Use Constraints to Fuel Creativity

1. **Reframe Constraints as Challenges**

   Instead of viewing limits as problems, treat them as opportunities to innovate.

2. **Simplify the Problem**

   Ask, "What's the simplest way to achieve this goal within these constraints?"

3. **Prioritize What Matters**

   Focus your energy on the most critical aspects of the problem or project.

4. Think Outside the Box

Explore unconventional ideas that wouldn't have been necessary without the constraint.

5. Learn from Minimalist Success Stories

Look at examples of businesses or individuals who thrived with limited resources.

A Real-Life Example

The Apollo 13 mission turned life-threatening constraints into ingenious problem-solving. Engineers used only available materials onboard to build a CO_2 filter, saving the crew's lives.

Exercise

Identify a current project with significant constraints. Write down one creative solution that turns the limitation into an advantage.

Takeaway

Constraints inspire innovation. Embrace limits as opportunities to focus, prioritize, and create smarter solutions.

Chapter 98: Balance Rational and Creative Thinking

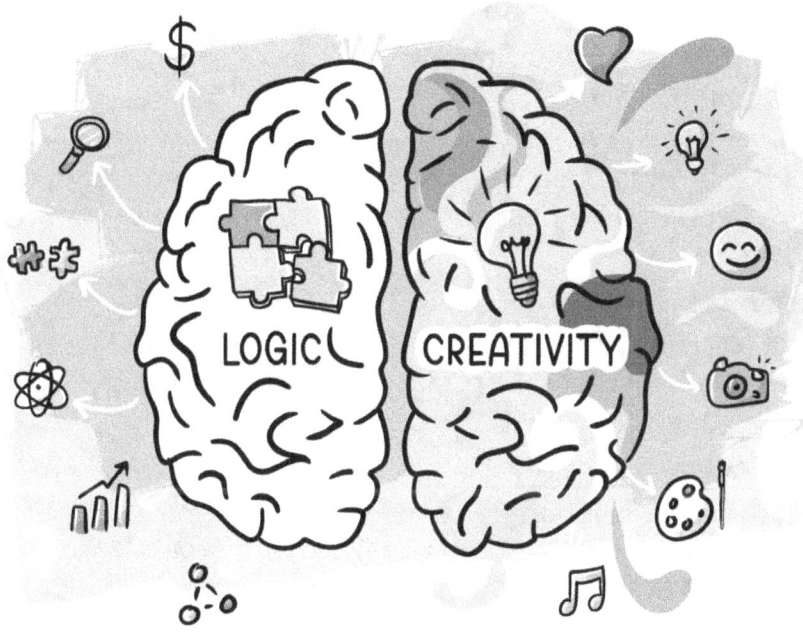

Effective problem-solving requires both rational thinking (logic, analysis) and creative thinking (imagination, innovation). Rationality ensures structure and accuracy, while creativity uncovers unique, outside-the-box solutions. Balancing the two unlocks your full problem-solving potential.

How to Balance Rational and Creative Thinking

1. **Start with the Problem**

   Use rational thinking to analyze the issue, gather data, and define clear goals.

2. **Brainstorm Freely**

   Switch to creative thinking to explore as many ideas as possible, even unconventional ones.

3. **Test and Refine Ideas**

   Return to rationality to evaluate and validate the feasibility of your creative solutions.

4. **Alternate Between Modes**

   Use rational thinking to structure your process and creative thinking to inspire new possibilities.

5. **Foster a Collaborative Team**

   Combine logical and imaginative thinkers to achieve a balanced approach.

A Real-Life Example

Steve Jobs combined rationality and creativity to design Apple products. Logical engineering ensured functionality, while imaginative design made them beautiful and user-friendly.

Exercise

Take a current problem and list two rational solutions and two creative solutions. Combine elements from each to create a balanced approach.

Takeaway

The best solutions come from blending logic with imagination. Balance rational analysis with creative thinking for smarter, more innovative outcomes.

Chapter 99: Build a Problem-Solving Framework

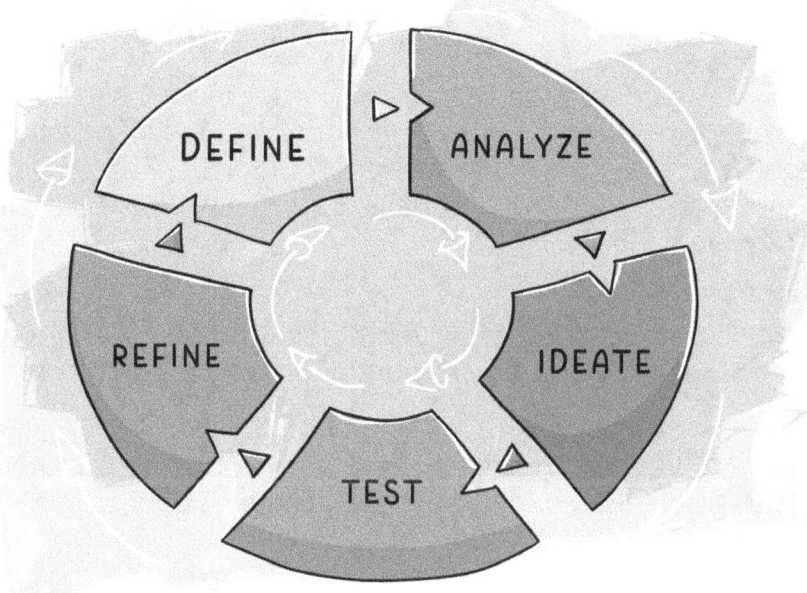

A problem-solving framework is a repeatable process that guides you from identifying a problem to implementing a solution. By using a framework, you eliminate guesswork, maintain focus, and improve efficiency. It's a tool that adapts to any challenge, providing structure and clarity.

How to Build and Use a Problem-Solving Framework

1. **Define the Problem**

   Clearly articulate the issue and its scope. Ask, "What's the real problem we need to solve?"

2. **Analyze the Situation**

   Gather data, identify root causes, and understand the context.

3. **Generate Ideas**

   Brainstorm multiple solutions, using techniques like mind mapping or the Five Whys.

4. **Test Solutions**

   Prototype or pilot your ideas to see what works best.

5. **Refine and Implement**

   Use feedback to improve your solution, then put it into action.

A Real-Life Example

Toyota's problem-solving framework, known as the Toyota Production System, focuses on identifying inefficiencies, testing improvements, and iterating solutions. This approach revolutionized manufacturing and inspired industries worldwide.

Exercise

Think of a recurring type of problem you face. Outline a five-step framework to handle it more effectively in the future.

Takeaway

A problem-solving framework provides structure and repeatability. Build one to approach challenges with confidence and clarity.

Chapter 100: Solve Problems Like an AI

AI solves problems systematically, breaking challenges into parts, analyzing data objectively, and iterating toward solutions. While humans add creativity and empathy, adopting an AI-inspired approach improves precision, efficiency, and clarity in problem-solving.

How to Solve Problems Like an AI

1. **Break the Problem Into Steps**

   Decompose the problem into smaller, manageable pieces.

2. **Analyze Data Objectively**

   Base decisions on evidence, not assumptions or emotions.

3. **Consider Multiple Scenarios**

   Evaluate potential outcomes for each solution to find the optimal path.

4. Iterate and Learn

Continuously refine your solution based on feedback and results.

5. Stay Consistent and Logical

Follow a structured approach to minimize errors and bias.

A Real-Life Example

Healthcare organizations use AI to optimize patient care. Algorithms analyze symptoms, test results, and treatment outcomes to recommend the most effective interventions, saving time and lives.

Exercise

Choose a problem and list the steps you'd take to solve it logically. Compare this process to how an AI might approach it, and note improvements you could make.

Takeaway

AI approaches problems with precision and objectivity. Adopt its systematic mindset to solve challenges efficiently and effectively.

Conclusion: The Endless Journey of Problem-Solving

Visual Suggestion for the Designer:

A winding path stretching toward the horizon, with signposts labeled "Learn," "Adapt," and "Grow." Along the path, a person holds a lightbulb, symbolizing continuous discovery and progress.

Problem-solving isn't a destination—it's a journey. From small daily decisions to transformative innovations, every problem is an opportunity to learn, adapt, and grow. This book has equipped you with 100 tools, techniques, and mindsets, but the real power lies in applying them to your unique challenges.

The world is constantly changing, and with it, the nature of problems evolves. That's why problem-solving requires both resilience and curiosity—resilience to tackle setbacks and curiosity to explore new solutions. Let's reflect on the key lessons from this journey and how you can keep improving as a problem-solver.

The Core Principles of Problem-Solving

1. Clarity is Key

Many problems feel overwhelming because they aren't clearly defined. Always start by asking, "What's the real problem?" Clear definitions lead to focused solutions.

2. Think Before You Act

Rushing to fix something without understanding its root cause often creates more issues. Tools like the Five Whys or Root Cause Analysis help you dig deeper before taking action.

3. Embrace Creativity and Logic

Problem-solving thrives on balance. Use logic to structure your process, but don't shy away from creativity to uncover innovative ideas.

4. Iterate, Learn, Repeat

No solution is perfect on the first try. Experiment, gather feedback, and refine your approach. Treat every attempt as a learning experience.

5. Stay Resilient

Setbacks are inevitable. The best problem-solvers view failure as a stepping stone, not a roadblock. Build resilience by focusing on growth and maintaining patience during uncertainty.

How to Keep Growing as a Problem-Solver

1. Practice Daily

Every decision you make is an opportunity to sharpen your problem-solving skills. From personal dilemmas to professional challenges, approach each situation with intention.

2. Expand Your Toolkit

The 100 techniques in this book are just the beginning. Stay curious and keep exploring new methods, tools, and ideas from different fields.

3. Learn from Others

Great problem-solvers often collaborate, learning from diverse perspectives. Surround yourself with thinkers who challenge and inspire you.

4. Stay Adaptable

Problems rarely come in the form you expect. Keep an open mind, stay flexible, and be ready to adjust your approach as needed.

5. Reflect and Refine

After solving a problem, take time to reflect. What worked? What didn't? Continuous improvement is the hallmark of a master problem-solver.

The Big Picture: Why Problem-Solving Matters

Problem-solving isn't just about fixing what's broken—it's about creating better systems, improving lives, and shaping the future. Whether you're tackling a personal challenge, leading a team, or addressing global issues, effective problem-solving empowers you to make meaningful change.

By mastering these skills, you're not only solving today's problems but building the confidence and mindset to face tomorrow's uncertainties. Every problem solved brings new insights, and every insight builds a stronger foundation for future success.

Your Next Steps

1. Choose a Problem

Look around you—what's one problem you can tackle today? Start small but act decisively.

2. Apply What You've Learned

Use the techniques in this book to approach the problem systematically. Experiment, test, and refine until you find a solution.

3. Share Your Journey

Problem-solving is a skill that grows through teaching and collaboration. Share what you've learned with others and work together to solve bigger challenges.

A Final Thought

The ability to solve problems is one of humanity's greatest strengths. It's what drives progress, fosters innovation, and turns challenges into opportunities. As you continue your journey, remember that every problem—no matter how daunting—holds the potential for growth and transformation.

Keep learning. Keep experimenting. Keep solving.

Appendix A: Quick Reference Guide to Problem-Solving: An AI's Guide to 100 Techniques for Finding Real Solutions Where Humans Get Stuck

This appendix serves as a quick reference guide to the book's sections and chapters, summarizing the core lessons of each chapter in one sentence. Use it to revisit techniques, refresh your understanding, or find the right strategy for your current challenge.

Section 1: Foundations of Problem-Solving

Learn the core principles and mindsets that underpin effective problem-solving.

1. **Start with the Problem, Not the Solution** – Clearly defining the problem prevents wasted effort on irrelevant solutions.

2. **Ask the Right Questions** – The right questions unlock deeper understanding and better answers.

3. **Distinguish Symptoms from Root Causes** – Solve the real issue, not just the surface symptoms.

4. **Stay Curious, Not Defensive** – Curiosity opens the door to fresh insights and innovative solutions.

5. **Understand the Power of Perspective** – Viewing the problem from different angles reveals hidden opportunities.

6. **Embrace Uncertainty** – Uncertainty isn't a barrier; it's the starting point for discovery.

7. **Keep Emotions in Check** – Emotional control leads to clearer, more rational decision-making.

8. **Break Down Big Problems into Small Steps** – Tackling manageable pieces makes any challenge less daunting.

9. **Focus on What You Can Control** – Direct your energy toward the parts of the problem within your influence.

10. **Test Before Committing Fully** – Small experiments save time and prevent costly mistakes.

Section 2: Creativity in Problem-Solving

Learn techniques to generate ideas, spark innovation, and think outside the box.

11. **Brainstorm Like a Pro** – Generate a flood of ideas without judgment.

12. **Think Outside the Box** – Shift your perspective to uncover unconventional solutions.

13. **Use Analogies to Spark Ideas** – Borrow solutions from other fields to solve your problem.

14. **Combine Ideas for Breakthroughs** – Merging diverse concepts often leads to innovation.

15. **Play with "What If?" Scenarios** – Hypothetical situations inspire creative possibilities.

16. **Reverse Engineer the Solution** – Work backward from the desired outcome to find actionable steps.

17. **Challenge Conventional Wisdom** – Question norms to uncover hidden opportunities.

18. **Steal Like an Artist (Ethically)** – Adapt successful strategies from others to fit your needs.

19. **Diverge, Then Converge** – Explore freely, then refine your focus to the best ideas.

20. **Gamify the Process** – Turn problem-solving into a fun and creative game.

Section 3: Analytical Thinking

Master methods to analyze, compare, and evaluate problems with precision.

21. **Follow the Data Trail** – Use evidence and numbers to guide your decisions.

22. **Use Root Cause Analysis** – Dig deeper to uncover the true source of a problem.

23. **Find Patterns and Trends** – Recurring themes often hold valuable clues.

24. **Use Decision Trees for Clarity** – Map choices to identify the most logical paths forward.

25. **Apply Pareto's Principle (80/20 Rule)** – Focus on the small efforts that create the biggest impact.

26. **Test Your Hypothesis** – Validate assumptions through experimentation.

27. **Use Comparative Analysis** – Evaluate options side by side to make informed choices.

28. **Correlation vs. Causation** – Learn to distinguish meaningful relationships from coincidences.

29. **Solve for Variables** – Isolate unknowns to simplify and solve complex equations.

30. **Simplify the Math** – Breaking numbers down reveals the bigger picture.

Section 4: Strategic Approaches

Develop long-term strategies and systems for tackling complex problems.

31. **Plan Backward from Success** – Imagine your goal achieved and trace the steps to get there.

32. **Think Like a Chess Player** – Anticipate moves and plan several steps ahead.

33. **Leverage Opportunity Costs** – Weigh the trade-offs of every decision.

34. **Identify Key Leverage Points** – Focus on small changes that drive big results.

35. **Map the System (Systems Thinking)** – Understand how all parts of a system influence each other.

36. **Scenario Planning for Uncertainty** – Prepare for multiple possible futures to stay adaptable.

37. **Build in Redundancy** – Add safety nets to reduce risks and handle setbacks.

38. **Focus on Long-Term Impact** – Make decisions that deliver lasting value.

39. **Prioritize Quick Wins** – Solve easier problems first to build momentum.

40. **Think Incrementally** – Solve in stages, building one solution on top of another.

Section 5: Collaborative Problem-Solving

Harness the power of teamwork to achieve better solutions.

41. **Harness the Power of Teamwork** – Combine strengths and perspectives to solve faster.

42. **Listen Before Solving** – Fully understanding the issue leads to better solutions.

43. **Balance Diverse Perspectives** – Different viewpoints strengthen solutions.

44. **Build Consensus with Stakeholders** – Agreement from all parties smooths implementation.

45. **Use Structured Decision-Making** – Follow clear processes for better group decisions.

46. **Avoid Groupthink** – Encourage dissent and critical thinking for smarter outcomes.

47. **Delegate and Share Responsibility** – Divide tasks strategically to achieve more.

48. **Seek External Expertise** – Know when to bring in specialists for complex problems.

49. **Communicate Solutions Effectively** – Present ideas clearly to gain support.

50. **Resolve Conflicts Constructively** – Turn disagreements into opportunities for progress.

Section 6: Emotional Intelligence in Problem-Solving

Learn to manage emotions and use empathy for better problem-solving.

51. **Stay Calm Under Pressure** – Keep a clear head in stressful situations.

52. **Recognize Emotional Triggers** – Identify feelings that cloud your judgment.

53. **Reframe Negative Thinking** – Turn pessimism into constructive action.

54. **Empathy as a Problem-Solving Tool** – Understand the issue from another's perspective.

55. **Manage Stress for Clearer Thinking** – Stay sharp by controlling your emotional state.

56. **Practice Self-Awareness** – Understand your biases and how they affect decisions.

57. **Build Resilience** – Bounce back stronger after setbacks.

58. **Use Optimism Strategically** – Stay hopeful while remaining realistic.

59. **Respect Other Viewpoints** – Approach disagreements with an open mind.

60. **Stay Open to Feedback** – Let constructive criticism improve your approach.

Section 7: Tools and Techniques

Master practical tools to analyze problems, organize thoughts, and find solutions.

61. **SWOT Analysis Made Simple** – Assess strengths, weaknesses, opportunities, and threats for clarity.

62. **The Fishbone Diagram (Ishikawa)** – Visualize cause-and-effect relationships to pinpoint root causes.

63. **Use the Five Whys** – Uncover deeper issues by repeatedly asking "Why?" until the root cause emerges.

64. **Apply Design Thinking** – Solve problems by focusing on user needs and iterative solutions.

65. **Use Mind Mapping for Clarity** – Organize complex ideas visually to simplify and connect them.

66. **Decision Matrix for Tough Choices** – Compare options using weighted criteria for objective decisions.

67. **The Power of Prototyping** – Test ideas quickly and refine them through feedback.

68. **Experimentation for Answers** – Use trial and error to validate ideas and uncover the best approach.

69. **Heuristics for Speed** – Simplify complex decisions with rule-of-thumb shortcuts.

70. **Algorithms and Flowcharts** – Create step-by-step processes for efficient problem-solving.

Section 8: Overcoming Cognitive Biases

Learn to recognize and counter mental shortcuts that distort decision-making.

71. **Recognize Confirmation Bias** – Avoid seeing only evidence that supports your beliefs.

72. **Avoid the Sunk Cost Fallacy** – Let go of past investments that no longer serve you.

73. **Fight Availability Heuristics** – Base decisions on facts, not the easiest or most vivid memories.

74. **Control Anchoring Effects** – Don't let initial information overly influence your thinking.

75. **Beware of Overconfidence Bias** – Stay humble about what you don't know.

76. **Manage Decision Fatigue** – Avoid poor decisions by reducing mental overload.

77. **Combat Group Polarization** – Prevent teams from becoming overly extreme in their views.

78. **Recognize the Dunning-Kruger Effect** – Understand the limits of your expertise.

79. **Counteract Framing Effects** – Look beyond how information is presented to see the full picture.

80. **Balance Intuition with Analysis** – Combine gut instincts with hard data for better decisions.

Section 9: Resilience in Problem-Solving

Build the grit and adaptability needed to thrive in problem-solving.

81. **Learn from Failure** – Treat setbacks as lessons for future success.

82. **Pivot, Don't Quit** – Adjust strategies instead of abandoning your goals.

83. **Stay Adaptive to Change** – Be ready to shift gears when circumstances evolve.

84. **Build a Feedback Loop** – Use feedback to continuously refine and improve solutions.

85. **Recognize When to Let Go** – Know when to walk away from unsolvable or low-value problems.

86. **Embrace Experimentation** – Test and iterate ideas to refine your approach.

87. **Cultivate Patience in Uncertainty** – Stay persistent even when results aren't immediate.

88. **Keep Your Eye on the Goal** – Stay focused on the bigger picture despite distractions.

89. **Trust the Process** – Believe in your problem-solving framework and stay consistent.

90. **Celebrate Small Wins** – Use incremental victories to fuel momentum and motivation.

Section 10: Advanced Problem-Solving

Elevate your problem-solving skills with cutting-edge techniques and strategies.

91. **Apply Game Theory** – Use strategic thinking to anticipate others' actions and optimize outcomes.

92. **Master First-Principles Thinking** – Break problems down to their fundamental truths for innovative solutions.

93. **Leverage Bayesian Thinking** – Update your beliefs continuously based on new evidence.

94. **Use Scenario Analysis for Complexity** – Prepare for multiple possible outcomes to stay adaptable.

95. **Explore Contrarian Solutions** – Consider ideas that go against conventional wisdom.

96. **Think Like a Futurist** – Anticipate long-term trends and shifts to stay ahead.

97. **Use Constraints to Your Advantage** – Turn limitations into creative opportunities.

98. **Balance Rational and Creative Thinking** – Combine logic with imagination for optimal solutions.

99. **Build a Problem-Solving Framework** – Develop a repeatable process to tackle any issue.

100. **Solve Problems Like an AI** – Approach challenges systematically and with precision.

Appendix B: Summary of Sections and Chapters

Below is a concise summary of the book's sections and their respective chapters. Use this as a quick reference to navigate the topics and techniques covered in the book.

Section 1: Foundations of Problem-Solving

1. Start with the Problem, Not the Solution
2. Ask the Right Questions
3. Distinguish Symptoms from Root Causes
4. Stay Curious, Not Defensive
5. Understand the Power of Perspective
6. Embrace Uncertainty
7. Keep Emotions in Check
8. Break Down Big Problems into Small Steps
9. Focus on What You Can Control
10. Test Before Committing Fully

Section 2: Creativity in Problem-Solving

11. Brainstorm Like a Pro
12. Think Outside the Box
13. Use Analogies to Spark Ideas
14. Combine Ideas for Breakthroughs
15. Play with "What If?" Scenarios
16. Reverse Engineer the Solution

Section 3: Analytical Thinking

Section 4: Strategic Approaches

Section 5: Collaborative Problem-Solving

Section 6: Emotional Intelligence in Problem-Solving

Section 7: Tools and Techniques

Section 8: Overcoming Cognitive Biases

Section 9: Resilience in Problem-Solving

Section 10: Advanced Problem-Solving

Appendix C: Practice Scenarios – Applying Problem-Solving Techniques

This appendix provides practical scenarios to help you apply the techniques from this book. Each situation represents a real-world problem and challenges you to solve it using one or more strategies from the chapters. These exercises encourage you to think critically, creatively, and strategically while refining your problem-solving skills.

Scenario 1: Launching a New Product

Situation: Your company is preparing to launch a new product, but there's confusion among team members about the marketing strategy. Some want to focus on social media, while others argue for direct mail campaigns.

Challenge: Use **SWOT Analysis (Chapter 61)** and **Balance Diverse Perspectives (Chapter 43)** to identify your product's key strengths and opportunities and build a consensus around the best strategy.

Scenario 2: Decreasing Customer Retention

Situation: Over the past three months, your company's customer retention rate has dropped by 20%. Initial surveys indicate that customers are frustrated with customer service response times.

Challenge: Apply **Root Cause Analysis (Chapter 22)** and **Build a Feedback Loop (Chapter 84)** to determine what's causing the delays and develop an ongoing system to gather and act on customer feedback.

Scenario 3: Conflict in a Team

Situation: Two members of your team are in disagreement about how to prioritize a project's tasks. One values speed, while the other prioritizes thoroughness. Their inability to compromise is delaying progress.

Challenge: Use **Empathy as a Problem-Solving Tool (Chapter 54)** and **Resolve Conflicts Constructively (Chapter 50)** to mediate the conflict and align the team on shared goals.

Scenario 4: Budget Cuts at Work

Situation: Your department has been asked to cut 15% from its budget, but every expense feels essential to operations.

Challenge: Apply **Use Constraints to Your Advantage (Chapter 97)** and **Pareto's Principle (Chapter 25)** to identify non-critical expenses and refocus resources on the 20% of efforts that yield the greatest results.

Scenario 5: Reviving a Failing Project

Situation: A long-term project has failed to meet its objectives, and team morale is low. Leadership is considering whether to cancel it or pivot in a new direction.

Challenge: Use **Pivot, Don't Quit (Chapter 82)** and **Scenario Planning for Uncertainty (Chapter 36)** to evaluate whether the project has potential in a revised format and outline next steps.

Scenario 6: Personal Time Management

Situation: You feel overwhelmed by a growing list of personal and professional commitments. Deadlines are approaching, and you're unsure where to start.

Challenge: Use **Decision Matrix for Tough Choices (Chapter 66)** and **Prioritize Quick Wins (Chapter 39)** to create a clear plan of action and build momentum by tackling small, manageable tasks first.

Scenario 7: Improving Employee Performance

Situation: An employee who usually excels has started missing deadlines and delivering subpar work. They've mentioned feeling burned out but aren't sure how to get back on track.

Challenge: Apply **Stay Calm Under Pressure (Chapter 51)** and **Build Resilience (Chapter 57)** to provide support and work with the employee to develop a strategy for overcoming burnout and improving performance.

Scenario 8: Competing in a Crowded Market

Situation: Your small business is competing against larger companies with bigger budgets in the same market. You need a strategy to stand out and attract new customers.

Challenge: Use **Think Outside the Box (Chapter 12)** and **Leverage Opportunity Costs (Chapter 33)** to develop a unique value proposition and focus your efforts on cost-effective, high-impact strategies.

Scenario 9: A Stalled Creative Project

Situation: You're working on a creative project (e.g., writing, art, or design) but feel stuck and uninspired. The deadline is looming, and you need a way to break through the block.

Challenge: Apply **Play with "What If?" Scenarios (Chapter 15)** and **Gamify the Process (Chapter 20)** to spark fresh ideas and make progress in a fun, low-pressure way.

Scenario 10: Planning for Uncertain Economic Conditions

Situation: Your business relies on supply chains that are being disrupted due to economic uncertainty. You need to plan for the potential impact on your operations.

Challenge: Use **Scenario Analysis for Complexity (Chapter 94)** and **Build in Redundancy (Chapter 37)** to prepare for various outcomes and create backup plans.

Scenario 11: Resolving a Personal Disagreement

Situation: You've had a disagreement with a friend or family member, and tensions are high. You want to resolve the issue while maintaining a healthy relationship.

Challenge: Use **Respect Other Viewpoints (Chapter 59)** and **Reframe Negative Thinking (Chapter 53)** to approach the conversation constructively and find common ground.

Scenario 12: Scaling a Business

Situation: Your business has seen rapid growth, but this has caused inefficiencies in operations, and you're struggling to meet demand.

Challenge: Apply **Map the System (Chapter 35)** and **Algorithms and Flowcharts (Chapter 70)** to streamline operations and create processes that support scalability.

Scenario 13: Deciding Between Job Offers

Situation: You've received two job offers, both with appealing benefits, but they cater to different priorities in your career and personal life.

Challenge: Use **SWOT Analysis (Chapter 61)** and **Decision Matrix for Tough Choices (Chapter 66)** to evaluate your options and choose the one that aligns best with your goals.

Scenario 14: Rebranding a Product

Situation: A product in your lineup is underperforming. You're considering whether to update its branding, revise the product itself, or discontinue it entirely.

Challenge: Apply **First-Principles Thinking (Chapter 92)** and **Use Feedback Loops (Chapter 84)** to rethink the product's fundamentals and refine it based on customer input.

Scenario 15: Preparing for a Big Presentation

Situation: You have an important presentation that could influence a major decision, but the stakes are high, and you're nervous about how it will be received.

Challenge: Use **Simplify the Math (Chapter 30)** and **Communicate Solutions Effectively (Chapter 49)** to distill your ideas into clear, persuasive points and present them confidently.

How to Use These Scenarios

These scenarios are designed to help you put theory into practice. Start by choosing a situation that resonates with a current challenge in your personal or professional life. Read the challenge, reflect on the suggested techniques, and apply them step by step. As you work through each exercise, revisit the relevant chapters for deeper insights and tools to refine your approach. The more you practice, the sharper your problem-solving skills will become.

Appendix D: Problem-Solving Checklist

This problem-solving checklist is your go-to guide for tackling challenges systematically and effectively. It includes 16 essential steps to ensure you approach problems with clarity, creativity, and strategy. Each step is broken down into actionable bullet points to help you stay focused and organized. Whether you're solving a personal dilemma, a workplace issue, or a strategic challenge, this checklist will keep you on track.

1. Clearly Define the Problem

- Write down the problem in one sentence.
- Ask, "What's the real issue here?" to ensure you're solving the right problem.
- Confirm your understanding by discussing it with others involved.

2. Break It Down Into Smaller Parts

- Divide the problem into manageable pieces to avoid feeling overwhelmed.
- Prioritize the most urgent or impactful parts to tackle first.
- Focus on solving one piece at a time to build momentum.

3. Gather All Relevant Information

- Identify what you know and what you still need to learn.
- Use credible sources like data, reports, or expert opinions to fill in gaps.
- Stay objective and avoid letting assumptions cloud your understanding.

4. Question Your Assumptions

- List all the assumptions you're making about the problem.
- Ask, "What if this assumption isn't true?" and consider alternative perspectives.
- Use first-principles thinking to challenge norms and uncover new solutions.

5. Explore Multiple Perspectives

- Seek input from diverse stakeholders to uncover blind spots.
- Put yourself in the shoes of others affected by the problem.
- Consider how the problem looks from different angles (e.g., financial, operational, emotional).

6. Identify the Root Cause

- Use tools like the Five Whys or a Fishbone Diagram to trace the problem back to its source.
- Ask, "Am I solving a symptom or the underlying issue?"
- Focus your efforts on addressing the root cause for long-term solutions.

7. Brainstorm Solutions

- Generate as many ideas as possible without judging them initially.
- Encourage out-of-the-box thinking by asking "What if?" questions.
- Record all ideas, even the unconventional ones—they could inspire breakthroughs.

8. Prioritize the Best Options

- Evaluate potential solutions using criteria like feasibility, impact, and cost.
- Use a Decision Matrix to objectively compare your options.
- Focus on solutions that offer the highest value with the least risk.

9. Develop an Action Plan

- Outline the specific steps required to implement your chosen solution.
- Assign responsibilities and set deadlines for each task.
- Ensure everyone involved understands the plan and their role in it.

10. Test the Solution on a Small Scale

- Pilot your solution in a controlled environment before a full rollout.
- Gather feedback to identify strengths and areas for improvement.
- Use the results to refine your approach before scaling up.

11. Anticipate Obstacles

- Brainstorm potential challenges or risks that could arise during implementation.
- Develop contingency plans to address these obstacles.
- Monitor progress regularly to catch and resolve issues early.

12. Stay Flexible and Adapt

- Be ready to pivot if your initial plan isn't working as expected.
- Use feedback loops to refine your solution in real-time.
- Keep the end goal in mind but stay open to new approaches.

13. Communicate Clearly

- Share your solution and action plan with all stakeholders in simple, concise terms.
- Use visuals like flowcharts or presentations to enhance understanding.
- Invite feedback and address concerns to build consensus and support.

14. Measure Results

- Define success metrics to evaluate the effectiveness of your solution.
- Track progress using data, feedback, or benchmarks.
- Compare results against your goals and adjust as needed.

15. Reflect and Learn

- Analyze what worked well and what didn't during the problem-solving process.
- Document lessons learned to improve your approach for future challenges.
- Share insights with your team to foster collective growth and improvement.

16. Celebrate Success

- Acknowledge your progress and the contributions of everyone involved.
- Highlight both the big wins and the small milestones along the way.
- Use the momentum to inspire confidence and enthusiasm for future challenges.

Pro Tip: Always Keep a Beginner's Mindset

Approach each problem with curiosity and an open mind, no matter how experienced you are. The willingness to learn, adapt, and explore new ideas is what sets great problem-solvers apart.

This checklist is a comprehensive guide for tackling challenges step by step. Keep it handy for quick reference, and remember: the key to effective problem-solving lies in consistent practice and refinement!

Here's another book by Quinn Voss that you might like

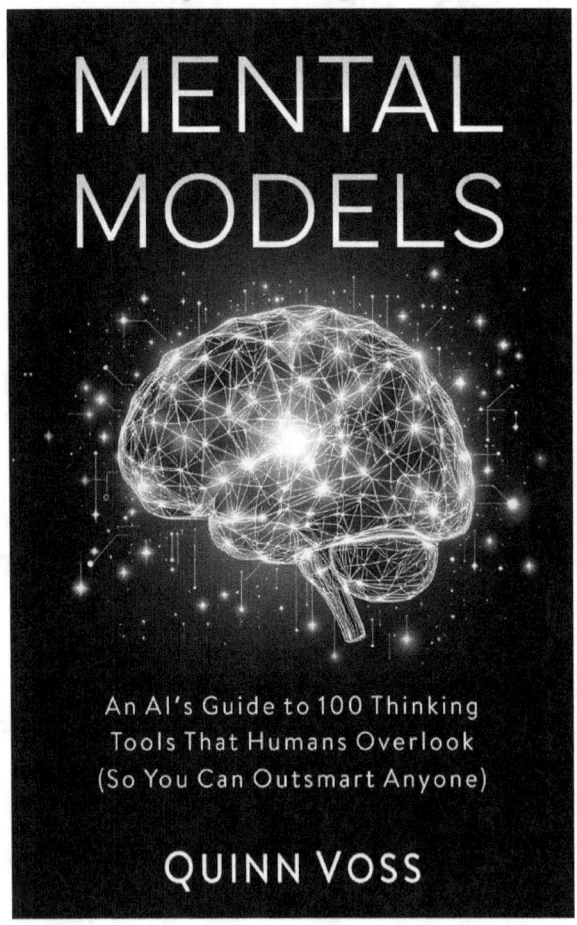

MENTAL
MODELS

An AI's Guide to 100 Thinking
Tools That Humans Overlook
(So You Can Outsmart Anyone)

QUINN VOSS